THE ART OF TRADING

Insider Tips for Stock Exchange Profits

Shah Rukh

CONTENTS

INTRODUCTION

The world of stock trading can be an exhilarating and potentially lucrative venture for those who possess the necessary knowledge and skills. However, navigating the complexities of the stock exchange and consistently making profitable trades is no easy task. To succeed in this dynamic and competitive field, traders must not only understand the fundamental principles of investing but also develop a unique set of strategies and techniques that can give them an edge in the market. This is where the art of trading comes into play.

"The Art of Trading: Insider Tips for Stock Exchange Profits" is a comprehensive guide that aims to equip aspiring traders with the insights, strategies, and insider tips necessary to navigate the stock exchange and maximize their profits. Drawing on years of experience and expertise from successful traders, this book serves as a roadmap for those seeking to master the art of trading.

In this book, we delve into the fundamental concepts of trading, providing a solid foundation for beginners to understand the mechanics of the stock market. We explain key terms, such as stocks, bonds, options, and futures, and explore the factors that influence stock prices and market trends. By demystifying the jargon and intricacies of the financial world, we enable readers to gain a clear understanding of how the market operates and the factors that drive its fluctuations.

Building upon this foundation, "The Art of Trading" delves into the strategies and techniques employed by successful traders. We explore various trading styles, including day trading, swing trading, and long-term investing, discussing the advantages and disadvantages of each approach. Through real-life case studies, we illustrate the application of these strategies, highlighting the importance of risk management, discipline, and emotional control in achieving consistent profitability.

One of the unique aspects of this book is its focus on insider tips and techniques employed by seasoned traders. We share insights into reading market indicators, analyzing technical charts, and identifying key patterns that can signal potential trading opportunities. Moreover, we discuss the role of fundamental analysis, including evaluating financial statements, understanding industry trends, and staying updated with economic news, in making informed investment decisions.

"The Art of Trading" also addresses the psychological aspects of trading, emphasizing the significance of developing a trader's mindset. We delve into the common pitfalls that traders encounter, such as fear, greed, and overtrading, and provide practical strategies for overcoming these challenges. By helping readers cultivate a disciplined and rational approach to trading, we aim to empower them to make informed decisions based on a solid understanding of the market dynamics.

Throughout the book, we emphasize the importance of continuous learning and adaptation in the ever-evolving world of trading. We discuss the role of technology in trading, including the use of algorithmic trading and automated systems, and highlight the need to stay updated with emerging trends and market innovations.

"The Art of Trading: Insider Tips for Stock Exchange Profits" is not a get-rich-quick scheme but a comprehensive guide designed to provide readers with the knowledge and tools they need to navigate the stock market successfully. Whether you are a novice trader looking to get started or an experienced investor seeking to refine your skills, this book is intended to be your go-to resource for honing your trading abilities and achieving consistent profitability in the exciting world of stock trading.

CHAPTER 1: THE FOUNDATIONS OF TRADING

1.1 Understanding the Stock Market

Understanding the stock market involves comprehending the basic concepts, mechanisms, and factors that drive the buying and selling of stocks or shares in publicly traded companies. It is a marketplace where investors can trade securities, such as stocks and bonds, issued by companies seeking capital to fund their operations or expansion.

Here are some key elements to consider when understanding the stock market:

1. Stocks: Stocks represent ownership in a company. When you buy shares of a company's stock, you become a partial owner and have a claim on its assets and earnings.

2. Stock Exchanges: Stock exchanges are platforms where stocks are bought and sold. Examples include the New York Stock Exchange (NYSE) and the NASDAQ. These exchanges provide a regulated environment for buyers and sellers to trade stocks.

3. Stock Indices: Stock indices, such as the S&P 500 or Dow Jones Industrial Average (DJIA), are benchmarks that measure the performance of a group of stocks. They help investors gauge the overall health and direction of the stock market.

4. Supply and Demand: The price of a stock is determined by the interaction of supply and demand. If more people want to buy a particular stock (demand) than sell it (supply), the price tends to rise. Conversely, if more people want to sell than buy, the price tends to fall.

5. Market Participants: Various participants contribute to the functioning of the stock market. They include individual investors, institutional investors (e.g., mutual funds, pension funds), traders, and market makers who facilitate the buying and selling process.

6. Fundamental Analysis: Fundamental analysis involves evaluating a company's financial health, performance, competitive position, and industry trends to determine its intrinsic value. Factors like earnings, revenue, debt levels, and management quality are considered in this analysis.

7. Technical Analysis: Technical analysis involves examining stock price and trading volume patterns to predict future price movements. It uses tools like charts, trend lines, and indicators to identify trends and patterns that can guide investment decisions.

8. Risk and Returns: Investing in stocks involve risks. Stock prices can be volatile, and there is no guarantee of positive returns. Investors need to carefully assess their risk tolerance and diversify their portfolios to manage risk effectively.

9. Long-Term Investing vs. Trading: Some investors adopt a long-term approach, aiming to benefit from the growth of companies over time. Others engage in short-term trading, attempting to profit from price fluctuations within a shorter time frame.

10. Economic and Market Factors: Economic indicators, geopolitical events, interest rates, and corporate news can significantly impact stock prices and market sentiment. Understanding these factors and staying informed about market developments is essential for successful investing.

It's important to note that investing in the stock market carries risks, and it's advisable to seek professional financial advice or conduct thorough research before making investment decisions.

1.2 Types of Traders

Traders are individuals or entities who participate in the buying and selling of financial instruments, such as stocks, bonds, commodities, or currencies, with the goal of making a profit. Different types of traders employ distinct strategies and time horizons to navigate the financial markets. Here are some common types of traders:

1. Day Traders: Day traders execute trades within a single trading day, aiming to profit from short-term price fluctuations. They often use technical analysis, charts, and indicators to identify patterns and make quick trading decisions. Day traders typically close their positions by the end of the trading day and rarely hold overnight positions.

2. Swing Traders: Swing traders hold positions for a few days to several weeks, capitalizing on medium-term price movements. They analyze both technical and fundamental factors to identify stocks or other assets with potential price swings. Swing traders may use strategies like trend following or momentum trading.

3. Position Traders: Position traders take longer-term positions in the market and hold them for weeks, months, or even years. They base their decisions on fundamental analysis, macroeconomic trends, and company-specific factors. Position traders often have a more patient and relaxed approach, seeking to capture substantial price moves over an extended period.

4. Scalpers: Scalpers aim to profit from small, rapid price movements by executing numerous trades within seconds or minutes. They rely on high-speed trading platforms and algorithms to take advantage of market inefficiencies. Scalping requires advanced technical

tools and a high level of focus.

5. Algorithmic Traders: Algorithmic traders use computer algorithms to automate trading decisions. These algorithms are designed to execute trades based on predefined rules, market conditions, and quantitative models. Algorithmic trading can be employed by various types of traders and can involve high-frequency trading or systematic strategies.

6. Options Traders: Options traders specialize in trading options contracts, which give them the right, but not the obligation, to buy or sell an underlying asset at a specified price within a set timeframe. Options traders may employ various strategies, such as buying and selling options, spreads, or combinations, to take advantage of price movements or hedge their positions.

7. Forex Traders: Forex traders focus on the foreign exchange market, where currencies are bought and sold. They speculate on the fluctuations in currency exchange rates, aiming to profit from these movements. Forex traders may use technical analysis, economic indicators, and geopolitical events to inform their trading decisions.

8. Commodity Traders: Commodity traders buy and sell physical commodities, such as oil, gold, natural gas, or agricultural products. They may trade futures contracts, options, or exchange-traded funds (ETFs) linked to specific commodities. Commodity traders analyze supply and demand factors, weather conditions, and global economic trends to make trading decisions.

It's worth noting that traders can overlap in their strategies and may adapt their approaches based on market conditions and personal preferences. Additionally, trading involves risks, and it's crucial for traders to manage their risk exposure, utilize proper risk management techniques, and stay informed about market developments.

1.3 Key Trading Terminologies

To understand trading, it's important to familiarize yourself with key terminologies used in the financial markets. Here are some essential trading terms explained:

1. Bid and Ask: The bid price represents the highest price a buyer is willing to pay for a security at a given moment, while the ask price is the lowest price at which a seller is willing to sell. The difference between the bid and ask prices is called the spread.

2. Market Order: A market order is an instruction to buy or sell a security at the prevailing market price. It ensures immediate execution but does not guarantee a specific price. Market orders prioritize speed of execution over price.

3. Limit Order: A limit order is an instruction to buy or sell a security at a specific price or better. It allows traders to set a price threshold at which they are willing to buy or sell. A buy limit order is executed at or below the specified price, while a sell limit order is executed at or above the specified price.

4. Stop Order: A stop order becomes a market order once the price of a security reaches a specified level, known as the stop price. A buy stop order is placed above the current market price and is triggered if the price rises to the stop price. A sell stop order is placed below the current market price and is triggered if the price falls to the stop price.

5. Stop-Loss Order: A stop-loss order is a type of stop order that is specifically used to limit potential losses. It is placed at a predetermined price level below the current market price (for long positions) or above the market

price (for short positions) to automatically sell or buy the security and minimize further losses.

6. Take-Profit Order: A take-profit order is an order to close a position and realize profits when the security reaches a predetermined price level. It is placed above the current market price (for long positions) or below the market price (for short positions).

7. Volume: Volume refers to the number of shares or contracts traded in a security or market during a given period. It indicates the level of activity and liquidity in the market. Higher volume often suggests increased interest and potentially greater price volatility.

8. Volatility: Volatility measures the price fluctuation of a security or market over a specific period. High volatility implies larger price swings, presenting both opportunities and risks for traders. Volatility is often calculated using statistical measures such as standard deviation or average true range.

9. Liquidity: Liquidity refers to the ease with which a security can be bought or sold without significantly impacting its price. High liquidity means there are sufficient buyers and sellers in the market, facilitating smooth and efficient trading. Low liquidity can lead to wider bid-ask spreads and potential difficulties in executing trades.

10. Margin: Margin refers to borrowing money from a broker to finance trading activities. It allows traders to amplify their buying power and potentially increase their returns. Margin trading involves using leverage but also carries higher risks, as losses can exceed the initial investment.

These are just a few key trading terminologies, and there are many more to explore. It's important to continue learning and familiarizing yourself with the language of trading to enhance your understanding of the markets and make informed trading decisions.

1.4 Importance of Risk Management

Risk management is a crucial aspect of any investment or trading activity. It involves identifying, assessing, and mitigating potential risks to protect capital and achieve long-term success. Here are the key reasons why risk management is essential:

1. Capital Preservation: Effective risk management helps preserve your capital and minimize the potential for significant losses. By employing risk management techniques, such as setting stop-loss orders or diversifying your portfolio, you can limit the amount of capital at risk in any single trade or investment.

2. Mitigating Emotional Biases: Emotions, such as fear and greed, can cloud judgment and lead to impulsive decision-making. Risk management strategies provide a structured framework to help control emotions and reduce the influence of emotional biases. By sticking to predefined risk parameters and plans, you can avoid making rash decisions based on short-term market fluctuations.

3. Consistent Performance: Consistency is key to long-term success in trading or investing. By implementing risk management practices, you establish a disciplined approach to your activities. This consistency allows you to focus on the quality of your trades and investments rather than being driven by sporadic and impulsive decisions. Over time, consistent risk management can lead to more reliable and predictable performance.

4. Balancing Risk and Reward: Risk management enables you to find an optimal balance between risk and reward. By assessing the potential risks of a trade or investment, you can determine if the potential reward justifies

taking on that risk. It helps you avoid excessive risk-taking that could jeopardize your financial well-being.

5. Controlling Losses: Risk management involves setting predefined exit points and stop-loss orders, which limit the amount you are willing to lose on a trade. By effectively managing your risk, you can control and contain losses, preventing them from spiraling out of control. This is crucial for long-term profitability and capital preservation.

6. Adaptation to Changing Market Conditions: The financial markets are dynamic and subject to constant change. Risk management techniques allow you to adapt to evolving market conditions and adjust your strategies accordingly. It helps you identify and respond to changing trends, volatility, or unforeseen events, enabling you to make informed decisions and mitigate potential losses.

7. Enhancing Risk-Reward Ratio: Risk management practices enable you to evaluate and improve your risk-reward ratio. By identifying opportunities with favorable risk-reward profiles, you can allocate your capital more efficiently and maximize potential returns while keeping risk exposure within acceptable limits.

8. Peace of Mind: Having a well-defined risk management plan in place provides peace of mind. It reduces anxiety and stress associated with trading or investing by providing a sense of control and structure. Knowing that you have strategies in place to manage potential risks can help you stay focused and confident in your decision-making.

In summary, risk management is of utmost importance in trading and investing. It protects your capital, helps you make consistent and informed decisions, controls losses, and ensures long-term profitability. By implementing sound risk management practices, you can navigate the markets with greater confidence and achieve your financial goals while minimizing the potential downsides.

1.5 Setting Realistic Goals

Setting realistic goals is a crucial aspect of personal and professional development. It involves establishing achievable objectives that align with your abilities, resources, and timeframe. Here's why setting realistic goals is important:

1. Motivation and Focus: Realistic goals provide a sense of direction and purpose. When your goals are attainable, you are more likely to stay motivated and focused on taking the necessary actions to achieve them. Achieving smaller milestones along the way can fuel your motivation, leading to continued progress.

2. Clarity and Vision: Setting realistic goals helps clarify your vision and define what you truly want to achieve. It allows you to break down your aspirations into specific, actionable steps. This clarity enables you to prioritize your efforts and allocate resources effectively.

3. Measurement and Progress Tracking: Realistic goals are measurable and tangible, making it easier to track your progress. By setting clear targets, you can regularly assess how far you've come and make adjustments if needed. Tracking progress provides a sense of accomplishment and allows you to identify areas where you need to put in more effort.

4. Avoiding Overwhelm and Burnout: Unrealistic goals can lead to overwhelm and burnout. When you set goals that are too ambitious or require resources beyond your reach, it can be demotivating and create unnecessary stress. Realistic goals, on the other hand, ensure that your efforts are aligned with your capabilities, reducing the risk of burnout.

5. Building Confidence: Achieving realistic goals builds confidence and self-belief. Each accomplishment reinforces the belief in your abilities and propels you forward. As you meet realistic targets, you gain confidence to take on more significant challenges and expand your capabilities.

6. Flexibility and Adaptability: Realistic goals allow for flexibility and adaptability in the face of changing circumstances. Life is unpredictable, and being able to adjust your goals as needed ensures that you stay on track despite unexpected events or challenges. Realistic goals are adaptable to accommodate new information, feedback, or changes in priorities.

7. Sustainable Progress: Realistic goals promote sustainable progress over the long term. By setting achievable objectives, you can maintain a steady pace of growth and improvement without risking burnout or giving up due to frustration. Sustainable progress allows you to develop habits and skills that support long-term success.

8. Celebrating Achievements: Realistic goals provide opportunities for celebration and acknowledgment of achievements. When you set attainable milestones, you can celebrate each step along the way, boosting your motivation and enjoyment of the journey.

To set realistic goals, consider factors such as your current abilities, available resources, time constraints, and potential challenges. Break down larger goals into smaller, manageable tasks, and set specific timelines. Regularly review and adjust your goals as needed to ensure they remain realistic and aligned with your evolving circumstances.

Remember, setting realistic goals does not mean settling for mediocrity. It means setting targets that stretch your capabilities while remaining within the realm of possibility. By setting realistic goals, you increase the likelihood of success, maintain motivation, and build a solid foundation for continuous growth and achievement.

CHAPTER 2: DEVELOPING A TRADING PLAN

2.1 Creating a Trading Strategy

Creating a trading strategy involves developing a systematic plan of action that guides your trading decisions and actions in the financial markets. A well-designed trading strategy helps you identify potential trading opportunities, manage risk, and make consistent and informed decisions. Here are the key steps involved in creating a trading strategy:

1. Define Your Trading Goals: Start by clarifying your objectives and what you aim to achieve through trading. Are you seeking short-term profits or long-term capital growth? Are you focused on a specific asset class or market? Defining your goals will shape the overall direction and focus of your trading strategy.

2. Choose a Trading Style: Determine your preferred trading style based on your personality, risk tolerance, and time commitment. Common trading styles include day trading, swing trading, position trading, or a combination thereof. Each style has its own characteristics and requires different time horizons and approaches.

3. Conduct Market Analysis: Analyze the financial markets and identify potential opportunities based on your chosen trading style. Use both fundamental analysis (evaluating economic indicators, company financials, and news events) and technical analysis (examining price patterns, trends, and indicators) to identify favorable trade setups.

4. Set Entry and Exit Criteria: Define specific criteria for

entering and exiting trades. Determine the conditions that must be met for you to initiate a trade, such as a certain price level, pattern formation, or fundamental indicator. Similarly, establish criteria for exiting trades, such as profit targets or stop-loss levels. This ensures that your trading decisions are based on objective criteria rather than emotions.

5. Implement Risk Management Measures: Develop a risk management plan that outlines how you will manage and mitigate risk. Determine your position sizing (how much capital you allocate to each trade), risk-to-reward ratios, and stop-loss levels. Risk management measures are crucial for preserving capital and limiting potential losses.

6. Test and Refine Your Strategy: Before applying your strategy with real money, test it using historical data or in a simulated trading environment. This allows you to evaluate its performance, identify strengths and weaknesses, and make necessary adjustments. Continuously refine and adapt your strategy based on market conditions and feedback from your trading experiences.

7. Maintain Discipline and Emotional Control: Emotions can have a significant impact on trading decisions. Establish rules for yourself and commit to following your strategy consistently, even during periods of losses or when faced with tempting opportunities outside your defined parameters. Emotional discipline is essential for maintaining a consistent approach and avoiding impulsive decisions.

8. Monitor and Evaluate Performance: Regularly assess the performance of your trading strategy and make adjustments as needed. Track key performance metrics such as win rate, average return per trade, and

maximum drawdown. Identify areas for improvement and learn from both successful and unsuccessful trades.

Remember that creating a trading strategy is an ongoing process. It requires continuous learning, adaptation, and refinement based on market conditions and your own experiences. As you gain more knowledge and insights, you can further enhance your strategy and increase your chances of trading success.

2.2 Fundamental Analysis

Fundamental analysis is a method used to evaluate the intrinsic value of an asset, such as stocks, bonds, or commodities, by analyzing the underlying factors that influence its value. It involves examining economic, financial, and qualitative factors to determine whether an asset is overvalued, undervalued, or fairly priced. Here are the key components and steps involved in fundamental analysis:

1. Economic Analysis: Fundamental analysis begins with assessing the overall economic environment. Factors such as GDP growth, inflation rates, interest rates, employment data, and geopolitical events can impact the performance of assets. Understanding the macroeconomic conditions provides a broader context for evaluating individual assets.

2. Industry Analysis: After analyzing the macroeconomic factors, focus shifts to the specific industry or sector in which the asset operates. Assessing the industry's growth prospects, competitive landscape, regulatory environment, and technological advancements helps determine the potential opportunities and challenges the asset may face.

3. Company Analysis: The next step involves evaluating the financial health and performance of the specific company associated with the asset. This analysis includes examining financial statements (such as

income statements, balance sheets, and cash flow statements), assessing profitability ratios, analyzing revenue and earnings growth, evaluating debt levels, and considering factors like management quality and corporate governance.

4. Valuation Techniques: Once the company's financials have been analyzed, various valuation techniques can be employed to estimate the asset's intrinsic value. Common valuation methods include price-to-earnings (P/E) ratio, price-to-sales (P/S) ratio, price-to-book (P/B) ratio, discounted cash flow (DCF) analysis, and comparable company analysis. These methods help determine whether the asset is overvalued or undervalued relative to its current market price.

5. Qualitative Factors: In addition to financial analysis, fundamental analysis also considers qualitative factors. These factors may include assessing a company's competitive advantages, intellectual property, brand reputation, market positioning, research and development capabilities, and management team. Understanding qualitative aspects provides insights into a company's long-term growth potential.

6. Market Sentiment: Fundamental analysis takes into account market sentiment and investor behavior. Factors such as market trends, analyst recommendations, and investor sentiment can impact the demand and pricing of assets. Evaluating market sentiment helps gauge whether the asset's price reflects market expectations or if there are potential discrepancies.

7. Risk Assessment: Fundamental analysis involves assessing both financial and non-financial risks associated with the asset. Factors such as regulatory changes, geopolitical risks, industry-specific risks,

and operational risks can impact the asset's value. Understanding these risks helps determine the overall risk profile of the investment.

8. Making Investment Decisions: After completing the fundamental analysis, the information gathered is used to make investment decisions. If the analysis suggests that the asset is undervalued relative to its intrinsic value, it may be considered a buying opportunity. Conversely, if the analysis indicates overvaluation, it may be a signal to sell or avoid the asset.

Fundamental analysis provides a comprehensive view of an asset's value based on various factors that drive its performance. It helps investors make informed decisions by considering the underlying financial and qualitative aspects that can impact an asset's price. However, it's important to note that fundamental analysis is just one approach to evaluating investments, and combining it with other methods can provide a more holistic perspective.

2.3 Technical Analysis

Technical analysis is a method used to evaluate investments by analyzing historical market data, primarily focusing on price and volume patterns. It aims to forecast future price movements and identify trading opportunities by studying market trends, patterns, and indicators. Here are the key components and principles of technical analysis:

1. Price Patterns: Technical analysis examines price patterns on charts to identify trends, reversals, and consolidation phases. Common patterns include support and resistance levels, trendlines, chart patterns (such as triangles, head and shoulders, and double tops/bottoms), and candlestick patterns. These patterns help traders predict future price movements based on historical price behavior.

2. Indicators: Technical analysts use indicators to provide additional insights into market trends and conditions. Indicators are mathematical calculations based on price and/or volume data. They can be classified into trend-following indicators (such as moving averages and trend lines) and oscillators (such as relative strength index (RSI) and stochastic oscillator), which help identify overbought or oversold conditions.

3. Volume Analysis: Volume is a crucial component in technical analysis as it provides insights into market activity and the strength of price movements. Changes in volume levels can confirm or contradict price trends, indicating the presence of buying or selling pressure. Volume analysis helps traders gauge market participation and the sustainability of price movements.

4. Trend Analysis: Technical analysis focuses on identifying and following market trends, which can be classified as uptrends, downtrends, or sideways (consolidation) trends. Trend analysis helps traders determine the direction in which prices are moving and allows them to align their trading strategies accordingly. Trend lines, moving averages, and trend-following indicators are commonly used to identify and confirm trends.

5. Support and Resistance Levels: Support and resistance levels are price levels were buying or selling pressure tends to be significant. Support levels are price levels at which buying interest is expected to emerge, preventing prices from falling further. Resistance levels, on the other hand, are price levels where selling pressure tends to increase, preventing prices from rising further. Traders use support and resistance levels to identify potential entry and exit points.

6. Risk Management: Technical analysis incorporates risk

management principles to protect capital and limit potential losses. This includes setting stop-loss orders, which define the maximum loss a trader is willing to tolerate on a trade, as well as determining position sizes based on risk-to-reward ratios. Risk management is essential to preserve capital and maintain consistency in trading.

7. Timeframes: Technical analysis can be applied to various timeframes, ranging from intraday charts to long-term charts. Traders use different timeframes based on their trading style and objectives. Short-term traders may focus on shorter timeframes (e.g., minutes or hours), while long-term investors may analyze daily, weekly, or monthly charts to identify long-term trends and patterns.

8. Limitations: It's important to note that technical analysis has its limitations. It does not consider fundamental factors or external events that may impact asset prices. Additionally, historical patterns and indicators may not always accurately predict future price movements. Therefore, combining technical analysis with other forms of analysis, such as fundamental analysis or market sentiment analysis, can provide a more comprehensive view.

Technical analysis is widely used by traders and investors to make informed decisions about buying, selling, or holding assets. By studying historical price patterns, indicators, and volume, technical analysis aims to identify trends and patterns that can provide insights into future price movements. It serves as a valuable tool for timing trades, managing risk, and formulating trading strategies.

2.4 Selecting Stocks for Trading

Selecting stocks for trading involves the process of identifying and choosing specific stocks that have the potential to generate profitable trading opportunities. Here are some key factors and considerations to keep in mind when selecting stocks for trading:

1. Trading Strategy Alignment: Start by aligning your stock selection with your trading strategy. Different trading strategies require different types of stocks. For example, if you are a day trader, you may focus on stocks with high liquidity and volatility, whereas a long-term investor may prioritize stocks with strong fundamentals and growth potential. Ensure that the stocks you choose are compatible with your trading style and objectives.

2. Fundamental Analysis: Conduct fundamental analysis to evaluate the financial health and performance of the company behind the stock. Consider factors such as revenue growth, earnings, profit margins, debt levels, industry position, competitive advantage, and management quality. Fundamental analysis helps assess the intrinsic value and long-term prospects of a stock.

3. Technical Analysis: Apply technical analysis techniques to analyze price patterns, trends, and indicators for the selected stocks. Look for patterns such as breakouts, reversals, and chart formations that can indicate potential trading opportunities. Technical analysis helps identify entry and exit points, support and resistance levels, and potential price targets.

4. Market Trends and Catalysts: Monitor market trends and identify catalysts that can impact the stock's price. Consider factors such as economic indicators, industry

developments, news events, regulatory changes, or company-specific announcements. Understanding the broader market environment and potential catalysts can help anticipate price movements and trading opportunities.

5. Liquidity and Volume: Choose stocks that have sufficient liquidity and trading volume to ensure smooth execution of trades. Stocks with high liquidity tend to have tight bid-ask spreads, reducing the impact of transaction costs. Additionally, higher trading volume indicates active market participation, increasing the likelihood of finding buyers or sellers when you want to enter or exit a trade.

6. Risk Management: Assess the risk associated with the selected stocks. Consider factors such as price volatility, market sensitivity, and correlation with other assets in your portfolio. Diversify your stock selection to manage risk effectively and avoid overexposure to a single stock or sector.

7. Company News and Events: Stay informed about company-specific news, earnings reports, product launches, mergers, or acquisitions that can impact the stock's price. Significant news or events can create short-term trading opportunities, so staying updated on the latest developments is crucial.

8. Historical Performance and Patterns: Evaluate the historical performance of the stock to identify any recurring patterns or trends. Look for patterns such as seasonal trends, earnings reactions, or price behavior in specific market conditions. Historical analysis can provide insights into how the stock has behaved in the past and help anticipate potential future movements.

9. Monitoring and Review: Continuously monitor and review the performance of the selected stocks. Regularly

assess whether the stocks are meeting your trading objectives and adjust your portfolio if needed. Stay updated on news, market conditions, and any changes in the stocks' fundamentals that may impact your trading decisions.

Remember that stock selection for trading is subjective and can vary based on individual preferences, risk tolerance, and trading strategies. It's essential to conduct thorough research, analyze multiple factors, and adapt your stock selection process based on changing market conditions. By combining fundamental and technical analysis, staying informed, and employing sound risk management practices, you can increase your chances of selecting stocks that offer profitable trading opportunities.

2.5 Determining Entry and Exit Points

Determining entry and exit points is a crucial aspect of trading and involves identifying the optimal times to enter and exit a trade. Entry points refer to the price level or condition at which you initiate a trade, while exit points indicate when you should close the trade to secure profits or limit losses. Here are some approaches and factors to consider when determining entry and exit points:

1. Technical Analysis: Use technical analysis tools and techniques to identify potential entry and exit points. This includes analyzing price patterns, trendlines, support and resistance levels, chart formations, and technical indicators. Technical analysis helps identify favorable entry points when a stock's price is expected to rise or fall based on historical patterns and indicators.

2. Breakouts and Pullbacks: Look for breakout patterns when a stock's price moves above a significant resistance level or below a significant support level. Breakouts can indicate a potential upward or downward trend and may be used as entry points. Similarly, pullbacks occur

when the price retraces temporarily during an ongoing trend, providing an opportunity to enter the trade at a relatively better price.

3. Trend Confirmation: Confirm the direction of the trend before entering a trade. This can be done through trendlines, moving averages, or other trend-following indicators. For example, in an uptrend, you may look for a pullback to the rising trendline or moving average as a potential entry point to go long. In a downtrend, you may consider short-selling when the price rallies to a declining trendline or moving average.

4. Candlestick Patterns: Analyze candlestick patterns to identify potential entry and exit signals. Patterns such as bullish/bearish engulfing, hammer, doji, or morning/evening star formations can provide insights into market sentiment and potential reversals. These patterns can indicate entry points when they occur at key support or resistance levels.

5. Fundamental Analysis: Consider fundamental factors when determining entry and exit points, especially for longer-term trades. Evaluate company financials, industry trends, news events, and macroeconomic factors that may impact the stock's value. Fundamental analysis can help you identify undervalued stocks for entry or overvalued stocks for exit.

6. Risk-Reward Ratio: Assess the risk-reward ratio before entering a trade. Determine the potential profit target and compare it to the potential risk or loss if the trade goes against you. A favorable risk-reward ratio ensures that the potential reward justifies the risk taken. Set realistic profit targets based on historical price movements, support/resistance levels, or technical indicators.

7. Trailing Stops and Stop-Loss Orders: Implement trailing

stops and stop-loss orders to protect profits and limit losses. Trailing stops allow you to adjust your stop-loss level as the price moves in your favor, locking in profits while giving the trade room to breathe. Stop-loss orders are predetermined price levels where you exit the trade to prevent excessive losses. Place stop-loss orders based on support/resistance levels or technical indicators.

8. Time-Based Exits: Determine exit points based on a predefined time frame. For example, if you are a short-term trader, you may exit trades at the end of the trading day. If you are a long-term investor, you may hold the stock for a predetermined period or until certain fundamental conditions are met.

9. Monitoring and Adjustments: Continuously monitor your trades and adjust your exit strategy if necessary. Pay attention to market conditions, news events, and changes in the stock's fundamentals. If the original reasons for entering the trade are no longer valid, consider adjusting your exit point accordingly.

10. Practice and Experience: Developing a sense of timing for entry and exit points takes practice and experience. Keep a trading journal to record your trades and analyze their outcomes. Learn from both successful and unsuccessful trades to refine your entry and exit strategies overtime.

Determining entry and exit points is a dynamic process that requires a combination of technical analysis, fundamental analysis, risk management, and market awareness. It involves identifying favorable price levels, patterns, and conditions to enter a trade while considering profit targets, risk tolerance, and potential exit signals. By combining various analysis techniques and continuously evaluating the market environment, you can enhance your ability to determine effective entry and exit points for successful trading.

CHAPTER 3: CHARTING AND TECHNICAL ANALYSIS

3.1 Reading Stock Charts

Reading stock charts is a fundamental skill for traders and investors, as it provides valuable information about a stock's historical price movements and helps in making informed decisions. Stock charts visually represent the price and volume data of a stock over a specific time period. Here are key elements and concepts to understand when reading stock charts:

1. Timeframe: Stock charts can be displayed in various timeframes, such as daily, weekly, monthly, or intraday intervals (e.g., 15 minutes, 1 hour). The timeframe chosen depends on the trader's investment horizon and trading style.

2. Price Axes: Stock charts typically have two axes: the vertical axis represents the stock price, and the horizontal axis represents the timeframe. The price axis may be displayed in either linear or logarithmic scale, depending on the charting platform.

3. Line Charts: Line charts connect the closing prices of a stock over a given timeframe, forming a continuous line. Line charts provide a simple visual representation of the stock's price trend over time.

4. Bar Charts: Bar charts display a vertical line, or bar, for each time period, representing the high, low, open, and close prices of the stock. The top of the bar indicates the highest price reached during the period, while the bottom represents the lowest price. A small horizontal line on the left side of the bar represents the opening price, and a small horizontal line on the right side

represents the closing price.

5. Candlestick Charts: Candlestick charts are similar to bar charts but provide additional information in a more visual format. Each candlestick represents a specific timeframe and displays the open, high, low, and close prices. The body of the candlestick is filled or colored to indicate whether the stock price increased (bullish) or decreased (bearish) during the period. Candlestick patterns, such as doji, hammer, or engulfing patterns, can provide insights into market sentiment and potential price reversals.

6. Volume Bars: Stock charts often include a separate panel or bar chart that represents the trading volume for each time period. Volume bars show the number of shares or contracts traded during a given timeframe. High trading volume can indicate increased market interest and potential price volatility.

7. Trendlines: Trendlines are drawn on stock charts to connect a series of higher lows (an uptrend) or lower highs (a downtrend). Trendlines help identify the general direction of the stock's price movement and can be used to anticipate potential support and resistance levels.

8. Support and Resistance Levels: Support levels are price levels where buying interest is expected to emerge, preventing the stock price from falling further. Resistance levels, on the other hand, are price levels where selling pressure tends to increase, preventing the stock price from rising further. These levels can be identified by horizontal lines on the stock chart, where the price has historically reversed or stalled.

9. Technical Indicators: Stock charts often incorporate technical indicators, such as moving averages, relative strength index (RSI), or MACD (Moving Average

Convergence Divergence). These indicators provide additional insights into market trends, momentum, and potential entry or exit signals.

10. Chart Patterns: Chart patterns, such as triangles, head and shoulders, double tops/bottoms, or flags, can provide valuable information about future price movements. These patterns are formed by the stock's price and can indicate potential trend reversals or continuation.

When reading stock charts, it's essential to combine technical analysis with other forms of analysis, such as fundamental analysis and market research, to gain a comprehensive understanding of a stock's potential. Regularly monitoring and analyzing stock charts can help traders and investors make informed decisions based on historical price patterns and trends.

3.2 Identifying Trends and Patterns

Identifying trends and patterns in financial markets is a crucial aspect of technical analysis. Trends and patterns provide valuable insights into the direction and potential future movements of stock prices, enabling traders and investors to make informed decisions. Here's an explanation of how to identify trends and patterns:

1. Trends:
   - Uptrend: An uptrend occurs when a stock's price consistently moves higher, forming a series of higher highs and higher lows. It indicates a bullish market sentiment, with buyers dominating and driving the price upward.

   - Downtrend: A downtrend occurs when a stock's price consistently moves lower, forming a series of lower highs and lower lows. It indicates a bearish market sentiment, with sellers dominating and pushing the price downward.

- Sideways or Range-bound: A sideways or range-bound trend occurs when the price moves within a relatively narrow range, neither forming significant higher highs nor lower lows. It indicates a lack of clear directional bias in the market.

2. Trendlines:
   - Trendlines are drawn on price charts to visually connect a series of higher lows in an uptrend or lower highs in a downtrend. They help define the slope and direction of the trend.

   - In an uptrend, draw an upward-sloping trendline by connecting the successive higher lows. This trendline acts as potential support, indicating levels where buying interest may emerge.

   - In a downtrend, draw a downward-sloping trendline by connecting the successive lower highs. This trendline acts as potential resistance, indicating levels where selling pressure may increase.

3. Chart Patterns:
   - Chart patterns are formed by price movements and provide insights into potential future price action. Some commonly observed chart patterns include:
     - Head and Shoulders: A head and shoulders pattern consists of three peaks, with the central peak (head) being the highest and the other two (shoulders) lower. It indicates a potential trend reversal from bullish to bearish.

- Double Tops and Bottoms: Double tops form when the price reaches a resistance level twice and fails to break higher. Double bottoms form when the price reaches a support level twice and fails to break lower. These patterns suggest potential reversals.

- Triangles: Triangles are characterized by converging trendlines and indicate a period of consolidation before a potential breakout. They can be ascending (bullish), descending (bearish), or symmetrical (neutral).

- Flags and Pennants: Flags and pennants are short-term continuation patterns that form after a significant price move. They resemble a flag or pennant shape and indicate a pause before the price resumes its prior trend.

4. Moving Averages:

   - Moving averages are technical indicators that smooth out price fluctuations and help identify trends. The most commonly used moving averages are the simple moving average (SMA) and the exponential moving average (EMA).

   - A rising moving average can indicate an uptrend, while a falling moving average can indicate a downtrend. Crossovers between different moving averages (e.g., the 50-day and 200-day moving averages) can also provide signals of trend reversals.

5. Oscillators and Indicators:

   - Oscillators and indicators, such as the Relative Strength Index (RSI), Moving Average Convergence Divergence (MACD), or Stochastic Oscillator, can help identify overbought and oversold conditions in the market. They provide signals of potential trend reversals or continuation based on price momentum.

It's important to note that no single trend or pattern can guarantee future price movements. It's advisable to use a combination of technical analysis tools, along with other forms of analysis, such as fundamental analysis and market research, to increase the probability of making accurate predictions. Regularly monitoring and analyzing trends and patterns in price charts can help traders and investors stay informed and make well-informed trading decisions.

3.3 Key Technical Indicators

Key technical indicators are tools used in technical analysis to analyze price movements, identify trends, and generate trading signals. These indicators are mathematical calculations based on historical price and volume data. They help traders and investors make informed decisions about buying or selling assets. Here are some key technical indicators:

1. Moving Averages (MA): Moving averages smooth out price fluctuations and provide a visual representation of the average price over a specific period. The two main types are Simple Moving Average (SMA) and Exponential Moving Average (EMA). Moving averages help identify trends, support and resistance levels, and generate crossover signals when different moving averages intersect.

2. Relative Strength Index (RSI): RSI is a momentum oscillator that measures the speed and change of price movements. It oscillates between 0 and 100. RSI values above 70 indicate an overbought condition, suggesting a potential price reversal or correction. Values below 30 indicate an oversold condition, suggesting a potential price bounce or recovery.

3. Moving Average Convergence Divergence (MACD): MACD is a trend-following momentum indicator. It consists of

two lines: the MACD line and the signal line. When the MACD line crosses above the signal line, it generates a bullish signal, indicating a potential uptrend. Conversely, when the MACD line crosses below the signal line, it generates a bearish signal, indicating a potential downtrend.

4. Bollinger Bands: Bollinger Bands consist of three lines plotted on a price chart. The middle line is a moving average, and the upper and lower bands are calculated based on price volatility. Bollinger Bands help identify overbought and oversold conditions. When the price touches the upper band, it may indicate an overbought condition and a potential reversal. When the price touches the lower band, it may indicate an oversold condition and a potential bounce.

5. Stochastic Oscillator: The Stochastic Oscillator compares a security's closing price to its price range over a specific period. It consists of two lines: %K and %D. Readings above 80 indicate an overbought condition, suggesting a potential reversal. Readings below 20 indicate an oversold condition, suggesting a potential bounce.

6. Fibonacci Retracement: Fibonacci retracement is based on the Fibonacci sequence and helps identify potential support and resistance levels. Traders use Fibonacci levels, such as 38.2%, 50%, and 61.8%, to identify areas where the price is likely to reverse or consolidate.

7. Volume: Volume is not a specific indicator, but it is an important component in technical analysis. Volume measures the number of shares or contracts traded during a given period. High volume often accompanies significant price movements, indicating increased market interest and potential trend continuation or reversal.

8. Average True Range (ATR): ATR measures volatility and provides an indication of a security's average price range over a specific period. It helps set stop-loss levels and determine position sizes based on volatility.

9. Ichimoku Cloud: The Ichimoku Cloud is a comprehensive indicator that provides multiple signals for trend identification, support and resistance levels, and potential entry and exit points. It consists of various lines, such as the Tenkan-sen, Kijun-sen, Senkou Span A and B, and Chikou Span.

10. Parabolic SAR: Parabolic SAR (Stop and Reverse) is a trend-following indicator that helps identify potential entry and exit points. It appears as dots above or below the price chart, indicating potential trend reversals.

It's important to note that technical indicators should not be used in isolation but in conjunction with other forms of analysis, such as price patterns, trendlines, and fundamental analysis. Traders and investors often combine multiple technical indicators to confirm signals and increase the accuracy of their trading decisions. Additionally, it's important to consider the specific characteristics of each security and adjust the indicators' parameters accordingly. Regularly monitoring and analyzing technical indicators can help traders identify potential trading opportunities and manage risks effectively.

3.4 Fibonacci Retracement and Extension

Fibonacci retracement and extension are technical analysis tools used to identify potential levels of support and resistance in a price chart. They are based on the Fibonacci sequence, a mathematical series in which each number is the sum of the two preceding ones (e.g., 0, 1, 1, 2, 3, 5, 8, 13, 21, and so on). Traders use Fibonacci levels to anticipate price reversals, retracements, and extensions in financial markets. Here's an explanation of Fibonacci retracement and extension:

Fibonacci Retracement: Fibonacci retracement is used to identify potential levels where a price correction (retracement) is likely to end and the original trend may resume. The most commonly used Fibonacci retracement levels are 38.2%, 50%, and 61.8%. Here's how it works:

1. Identify the Swing Points: Identify a significant swing high and swing low on the price chart. The swing high represents a peak in the price, while the swing low represents a trough or bottom.

2. Draw Fibonacci Levels: With the swing high and swing low identified, draw horizontal lines at the Fibonacci retracement levels of 38.2%, 50%, and 61.8%. These levels act as potential support or resistance levels.

3. Interpretation:
   - When the price retraces and approaches a Fibonacci retracement level, it may find support or resistance. Traders often look for price reactions, such as trend continuation signals or candlestick patterns, around these levels to confirm potential entry or exit points.

   - If the price retraces beyond the 61.8% level, it may indicate a significant trend reversal or a deeper correction. Traders may consider this as a potential change in the overall trend direction.

Fibonacci Extension: Fibonacci extension is used to identify potential levels where the price may extend beyond its previous swing high or low. It helps traders identify possible target levels for profit-taking or price projections. The most commonly used Fibonacci extension levels are 127.2%, 161.8%, and 261.8%. Here's how it works:

1. Identify the Swing Points: Identify a significant swing high and swing low on the price chart, similar to the process for Fibonacci retracement.

2. Draw Fibonacci Levels: With the swing high and swing low identified, draw horizontal lines at the Fibonacci extension levels of 127.2%, 161.8%, and 261.8%. These levels act as potential price targets.

3. Interpretation:

- When the price moves beyond its previous swing high or low, it may encounter resistance or support near the Fibonacci extension levels.

- Traders may consider taking profits or scaling out of positions as the price approaches these extension levels, as they indicate potential areas where the price could reverse or consolidate.

It's important to note that Fibonacci retracement and extension levels are not foolproof indicators and should be used in conjunction with other technical analysis tools. They are subjective tools and their effectiveness can vary depending on market conditions. Therefore, it's crucial to combine them with other forms of analysis and consider additional factors such as trendlines, candlestick patterns, and volume to validate potential entry and exit points.

3.5 Candlestick Patterns

Candlestick patterns are a popular tool used in technical analysis to analyze price movements and identify potential trend reversals, continuations, or indecision in financial markets. Candlestick charts display the open, high, low, and close prices of an asset within a specific time period. Each candlestick represents a single period, such as a day, hour, or minute. Here's an explanation of candlestick patterns:

1. Anatomy of a Candlestick:

- Body: The rectangular area between the open and close prices. It is filled (colored) if the close price is lower than the open price, indicating a bearish sentiment. It is hollow (not colored) if the close price is higher than the open price, indicating a bullish sentiment.

- Wick (or shadow): The thin lines extending above and below the body. The upper wick represents the high price, and the lower wick represents the low price.

2. Bullish Candlestick Patterns:
   - Hammer: It has a small body at the upper end of the range with a long lower wick. It indicates potential bullish reversal after a downtrend.

   - Bullish Engulfing: It occurs when a larger bullish candle completely engulfs the previous smaller bearish candle. It suggests a potential bullish reversal.

   - Morning Star: It consists of three candles. The first is a bearish candle, followed by a small bullish or bearish candle, and finally a larger bullish candle. It indicates a potential bullish reversal after a downtrend.

3. Bearish Candlestick Patterns:
   - Shooting Star: It has a small body at the lower end of the range with a long upper wick. It suggests potential bearish reversal after an uptrend.

   - Bearish Engulfing: It occurs when a larger bearish candle completely engulfs the previous smaller bullish candle. It suggests a potential bearish reversal.

   - Evening Star: It consists of three candles. The first is a bullish candle, followed by a small bullish or bearish candle, and finally a larger bearish candle. It indicates a potential bearish reversal after an uptrend.

4. Reversal Patterns:
    - Doji: It has a small body with wicks of similar length, indicating indecision between buyers and sellers. It suggests a potential trend reversal or indecision in the market.

    - Tweezer Tops and Bottoms: They occur when two or more candlesticks have similar highs (tops) or lows (bottoms), indicating potential resistance or support levels.

5. Continuation Patterns:
    - Bullish and Bearish Flags: They are small rectangular patterns that occur after a strong price move. Bullish flags slope upward, while bearish flags slope downward. They indicate a potential continuation of the previous trend.

    - Symmetrical, Ascending, and Descending Triangles: These triangle patterns indicate a period of consolidation and indecision in the market, with converging trendlines. A breakout from the triangle can indicate a potential continuation of the previous trend.

6. Other Patterns:
    - Doji Star: It is a Doji pattern that gap away from the preceding candle, indicating potential trend reversal.

    - Harami: It occurs when a small candle is contained within the range of the previous larger candle. It suggests potential trend reversal or indecision.

It's important to note that candlestick patterns are not foolproof indicators and should be used in conjunction with other forms of analysis and confirmation. Traders often combine candlestick patterns with support and resistance levels, trendlines, and other technical indicators to increase the accuracy of their predictions. Regularly monitoring and analyzing candlestick patterns can help traders identify potential trading opportunities and make more informed trading decisions.

CHAPTER 4: FUNDAMENTAL ANALYSIS AND COMPANY RESEARCH

4.1 Understanding Fundamental Analysis

Fundamental analysis is a method of evaluating financial assets, such as stocks, bonds, and commodities, by examining the intrinsic value of the underlying asset. It involves analyzing various factors that can influence the value and performance of an asset, such as the overall economy, industry conditions, company financials, and market trends. The goal of fundamental analysis is to determine whether an asset is overvalued, undervalued, or fairly priced, and to make investment decisions based on this assessment.

Here are some key components and concepts of fundamental analysis:

1. Economic Analysis: Fundamental analysis begins with assessing the overall economic environment. Factors such as GDP growth, inflation rates, interest rates, employment data, and government policies can have a significant impact on the performance of financial assets. By understanding the broader economic conditions, investors can gain insights into the potential opportunities and risks associated with different investments.

2. Industry Analysis: After evaluating the macroeconomic factors, fundamental analysis focuses on analyzing the specific industry in which a company operates. Industry analysis involves studying the competitive landscape, market size, growth prospects, regulatory environment, technological advancements, and any other factors that

can affect the industry's profitability and outlook. This analysis helps investors identify industries that are poised for growth and those facing challenges.

3. Company Financials: The financial statements of a company, including the income statement, balance sheet, and cash flow statement, provide valuable information for fundamental analysis. Investors analyze key financial ratios, such as earnings per share (EPS), price-to-earnings (P/E) ratio, return on equity (ROE), and debt-to-equity ratio, to assess the company's financial health, profitability, efficiency, and leverage. By examining financial trends over time, investors can identify patterns and make predictions about future performance.

4. Qualitative Factors: In addition to financial data, fundamental analysis considers qualitative factors that can impact a company's prospects. This includes management quality and experience, corporate governance practices, brand reputation, product differentiation, competitive advantages, research and development capabilities, and market positioning. Qualitative analysis provides insights into a company's competitive strengths and potential risks that may not be evident from financial statements alone.

5. Valuation Methods: Fundamental analysis employs various valuation methods to determine the intrinsic value of an asset. Common valuation techniques include discounted cash flow (DCF) analysis, price-to-earnings (P/E) ratio, price-to-sales (P/S) ratio, and price-to-book (P/B) ratio. These methods help investors assess whether a stock is undervalued or overvalued relative to its intrinsic worth.

6. Event Analysis: Fundamental analysis also considers significant events or news that can impact the value

of an asset. This includes factors like mergers and acquisitions, product launches, regulatory changes, litigation, and macroeconomic events. Evaluating the potential impact of these events on a company's financials and market position is essential in understanding its future prospects.

Fundamental analysis is often used by long-term investors who seek to build a portfolio based on the underlying value of the assets. However, it can also be employed by traders to identify short-term trading opportunities. By combining fundamental analysis with other forms of analysis, such as technical analysis, investors can make more informed investment decisions. It's important to note that fundamental analysis has its limitations, and market prices can be influenced by factors beyond fundamental factors, such as market sentiment and investor behavior.

4.2 Evaluating Financial Statements

Evaluating financial statements is a critical aspect of fundamental analysis that involves analyzing a company's financial performance and position. Financial statements provide a snapshot of a company's financial health, including its revenues, expenses, assets, liabilities, and equity. By examining these statements, investors and analysts can gain insights into a company's profitability, liquidity, solvency, and overall financial stability. Here are the key components and concepts involved in evaluating financial statements:

1. Income Statement (Profit and Loss Statement): The income statement provides information about a company's revenues, expenses, and net income over a specific period. It helps assess the company's profitability and ability to generate earnings. Key elements of the income statement include:

   • Revenue: The total sales or revenues generated by

the company.

- Cost of Goods Sold (COGS): The direct costs associated with producing or delivering goods or services.

- Gross Profit: Revenue minus COGS, indicating the profitability from core operations.

- Operating Expenses: The costs incurred in running the day-to-day operations of the business.

- Operating Income: Gross profit minus operating expenses, representing the profitability before taxes and interest.

- Net Income: The final measure of profitability, representing the company's earnings after taxes and interest.

2. Balance Sheet: The balance sheet provides a snapshot of a company's financial position at a specific point in time. It shows the company's assets, liabilities, and shareholders' equity. Key elements of the balance sheet include:

- Assets: The resources owned by the company, such as cash, inventory, property, plant, and equipment.

- Liabilities: The company's debts or obligations, including loans, accounts payable, and accrued expenses.

- Shareholders' Equity: The residual interest in the company's assets after deducting liabilities. The balance sheet helps assess a company's liquidity (ability to meet short-term obligations) and solvency (ability to meet long-term obligations).

3. Cash Flow Statement: The cash flow statement tracks the flow of cash into and out of the company during a

specific period. It provides insights into the company's ability to generate and manage cash. Key components of the cash flow statement include:

- Operating Activities: Cash flows from the company's core operations, such as cash generated from sales and payments to suppliers.

- Investing Activities: Cash flows from buying or selling long-term assets, such as investments, property, plant, and equipment.

- Financing Activities: Cash flows from borrowing or repaying debt, issuing or buying back shares, and paying dividends. The cash flow statement helps assess a company's ability to generate positive cash flow, manage working capital, and fund its operations and investments.

4. Financial Ratios: Financial ratios are derived from the information in financial statements and provide a quantitative analysis of a company's performance and financial health. Some common financial ratios include:

- Profitability Ratios: Measures of a company's ability to generate profits, such as gross profit margin, net profit margin, and return on equity (ROE).

- Liquidity Ratios: Measures of a company's ability to meet short-term obligations, such as the current ratio and the quick ratio.

- Solvency Ratios: Measures of a company's ability to meet long-term obligations, such as the debt-to-equity ratio and interest coverage ratio.

- Efficiency Ratios: Measures of a company's efficiency in managing its assets and liabilities, such as inventory turnover and accounts receivable turnover.

By analyzing these financial statements and ratios, investors can gain insights into a company's financial performance, profitability, cash flow generation, and overall financial health. It's important to compare the financial statements of a company over time to identify trends, benchmark the company against its industry peers, and consider the company's business model and industry dynamics when interpreting the financial data. Additionally, it is often helpful to conduct ratio analysis and compare the financial performance of a company with industry standards and competitors to gain a broader perspective. Overall, evaluating financial statements is a crucial step in fundamental analysis, enabling investors to make informed decisions about investing in a particular company or industry.

4.3 Assessing Industry and Market Trends

Assessing industry and market trends is a vital part of conducting fundamental analysis and making informed investment decisions. It involves analyzing the broader economic, industry-specific, and market factors that can impact the performance and outlook of companies operating within a particular sector. Here's an overview of assessing industry and market trends:

1. Macroeconomic Factors:
    - Economic Growth: Evaluate the overall economic conditions, such as GDP growth, inflation rates, interest rates, and consumer spending. Strong economic growth can benefit most industries, while a slowdown can have a negative impact.

    - Government Policies: Assess the impact of government regulations, fiscal policies, trade policies, and changes in taxation on the industry. Regulatory changes or government incentives can significantly influence industry dynamics.

- Global Factors: Consider global economic trends, geopolitical events, and international trade policies that can impact the industry's performance, especially if the industry is globally interconnected.

2. Industry Analysis:
    - Market Size and Growth: Understand the current market size and the potential for growth in the industry. Analyze historical growth rates and forecasted trends to identify sectors with strong growth prospects.

    - Competitive Landscape: Evaluate the level of competition within the industry, including the market share of major players, entry barriers, and the threat of new entrants or substitutes. Assess the competitive advantages of companies within the industry.

    - Technological Advancements: Consider the impact of technological advancements and innovation on the industry. Industries that adapt and leverage new technologies often have a competitive edge.

    - Regulatory Environment: Assess the regulatory framework and compliance requirements that impact the industry. Changes in regulations can create opportunities or pose challenges for companies.

    - Supply and Demand Dynamics: Analyze the balance between supply and demand in the industry. Examine factors such as production capacity, inventory levels, and pricing power.

    - Industry Cycles: Understand the typical

industry cycles, including periods of expansion, consolidation, and decline. Identify the current stage of the industry cycle and anticipate future trends.

3. Market Analysis:

- Investor Sentiment: Monitor investor sentiment and market psychology, as it can influence the overall market trends. Factors like market optimism, fear, and risk appetite can impact investment decisions and market movements.

- Market Indices: Track relevant market indices, such as stock market indices or sector-specific indices, to gauge the overall market performance and trends.

- Market Volatility: Assess the level of market volatility and its potential impact on industry stocks. Volatile markets can present both opportunities and risks.

- Market Trends: Identify broader market trends, such as shifts in consumer preferences, emerging technologies, or demographic changes, that can create new opportunities or disrupt existing industries.

- Market Research and Reports: Stay informed through market research reports, industry publications, analyst insights, and news updates specific to the industry or market segment.

By assessing industry and market trends, investors can identify sectors with strong growth potential, understand the competitive landscape, and make informed investment decisions. It is important to combine industry and market analysis with company-specific analysis to get a comprehensive view of the investment opportunities and risks. Regular monitoring of industry and market trends is essential to adapt investment strategies to changing conditions and identify potential shifts in the investment landscape.

4.4 Analyzing Company Management and Governance

Analyzing company management and governance is an important aspect of fundamental analysis that helps investors assess the competence, integrity, and effectiveness of a company's leadership. The management team plays a crucial role in shaping the company's strategic direction, making operational decisions, and creating long-term value for shareholders. Here's an overview of analyzing company management and governance:

1. Management Team Assessment:
   - Qualifications and Experience: Evaluate the qualifications and experience of key executives, including the CEO, CFO, and other top-level managers. Assess their educational background, industry expertise, and track record in managing similar companies or projects.
   - Leadership Style: Consider the leadership style and approach of the management team. Assess their ability to inspire and motivate employees, foster innovation, and navigate challenges.
   - Corporate Culture: Evaluate the company's corporate culture as influenced by its management. Consider factors such as transparency, accountability, employee engagement, and commitment to ethical practices.
   - Succession Planning: Assess whether the company has a robust succession plan in place. A well-defined plan ensures smooth transitions

and continuity in leadership, reducing uncertainty and risks for investors.

2. Board of Directors:
   - Composition: Evaluate the composition of the company's board of directors. Consider the independence of directors, their expertise in relevant areas, diversity, and their ability to provide effective oversight of management.

   - Board Structure: Assess whether the board has appropriate committees (e.g., audit committee, compensation committee) to oversee critical areas. Evaluate the frequency and effectiveness of board meetings and the level of engagement with management.

   - Related Party Transactions: Scrutinize any related party transactions to ensure they are conducted at arm's length and are in the best interest of shareholders.

   - Corporate Governance Policies: Evaluate the company's corporate governance policies, codes of conduct, and compliance mechanisms. Strong governance policies promote transparency, accountability, and ethical behavior.

3. Financial Reporting and Transparency:
   - Financial Disclosures: Assess the quality and transparency of the company's financial reporting. Look for clear and comprehensive disclosures in financial statements, footnotes, and accompanying documents.

   - Auditing and External Oversight: Evaluate the company's relationship with independent auditors and external oversight bodies. Consider the reputation and independence of the auditing firm and the level of scrutiny applied to financial statements.

- Risk Management: Assess the company's risk management practices and internal controls. Look for evidence of robust risk assessment, mitigation strategies, and a culture of risk awareness within the organization.

4. Shareholder Relations:
    - Shareholder Communication: Evaluate the company's approach to shareholder communication and engagement. Consider whether the company provides regular updates, holds shareholder meetings, and responds to shareholder concerns.

    - Dividend Policy: Assess the company's dividend policy and its commitment to returning value to shareholders. Evaluate the consistency and sustainability of dividend payments.

    - Executive Compensation: Review the company's executive compensation policies and practices. Assess whether executive compensation is aligned with company performance and shareholder interests.

Analyzing company management and governance helps investors gain confidence in the company's ability to effectively manage operations, navigate challenges, and create long-term value. It is important to consider both qualitative and quantitative factors and to compare the company's practices with industry peers and best practices. Strong management and governance practices can contribute to a company's sustainable growth, mitigate risks, and protect shareholder interests.

4.5 Incorporating Economic Indicators and News Analysis

Incorporating economic indicators and news analysis is an important aspect of both fundamental and macroeconomic analysis. It involves monitoring and analyzing various economic indicators and staying informed about relevant news events to gain insights into the overall economic conditions and their potential impact on financial markets. Here's an overview of incorporating economic indicators and news analysis in investment decision-making:

1. Economic Indicators:
   - GDP Growth: Gross Domestic Product (GDP) measures the overall economic activity of a country. It indicates the rate of economic growth or contraction and provides insights into the health of the economy.

   - Employment Data: Key employment indicators, such as the unemployment rate, non-farm payrolls, and jobless claims, provide insights into the labor market conditions. Strong employment data is generally indicative of a healthy economy.

   - Inflation Measures: Consumer Price Index (CPI) and Producer Price Index (PPI) track changes in the prices of goods and services. Inflation can impact interest rates, consumer spending, and the overall purchasing power of consumers.

   - Interest Rates: Central bank interest rate decisions, such as those made by the Federal Reserve in the US or the European Central Bank in the Eurozone, can have a significant impact on borrowing costs, investment decisions, and currency valuations.

   - Consumer Confidence: Measures of consumer sentiment, such as consumer confidence indexes, reflect consumers' perception of the overall economic conditions. Consumer spending plays a vital role in driving economic growth.

- Business Confidence: Business surveys and sentiment indicators, such as the Purchasing Managers' Index (PMI), provide insights into the outlook for business activity and investment.

2. News Analysis:

- Monetary Policy Announcements: Central bank decisions and statements regarding interest rates, quantitative easing, or other policy measures can have a significant impact on financial markets. Analyzing these announcements helps gauge the direction of monetary policy and its implications for the economy and markets.

- Fiscal Policy Developments: Government policies related to taxes, government spending, and stimulus measures can influence economic growth and market sentiment. News about fiscal policy changes can provide insights into potential market impacts.

- Geopolitical Events: Political developments, international conflicts, and trade disputes can create volatility and uncertainty in financial markets. Analyzing geopolitical news helps identify potential risks and opportunities.

- Industry-specific News: Monitoring news related to specific industries or sectors helps investors understand the latest trends, regulatory changes, technological advancements, and competitive dynamics that may impact specific companies or sectors.

- Company-specific News: News related to individual companies, such as earnings releases, product launches, mergers and acquisitions, or legal issues, can significantly impact stock prices and investor sentiment. Analyzing company-specific news helps assess the fundamental factors driving individual stock performance.

Incorporating economic indicators and news analysis allows investors to gain a broader perspective on the overall economic climate, industry trends, and market sentiment. By understanding how economic factors and news events can impact financial markets, investors can make more informed investment decisions. It is important to analyze both the quantitative data provided by economic indicators and the qualitative aspects of news analysis to form a comprehensive view. Regular monitoring of economic indicators and staying up-to-date with relevant news events is crucial for adapting investment strategies to changing market conditions.

CHAPTER 5: RISK MANAGEMENT AND MONEY MANAGEMENT

5.1 The Importance of Risk Management

The importance of risk management cannot be overstated when it comes to investing and trading. Risk management refers to the process of identifying, assessing, and mitigating potential risks to protect capital and minimize losses. It is a fundamental component of any successful investment strategy. Here are the key reasons why risk management is crucial:

1. Capital Preservation: The primary goal of risk management is to protect capital. By implementing risk management strategies, investors aim to minimize the potential for significant losses. Preserving capital is essential for long-term investment success as it ensures the availability of funds for future investment opportunities.

2. Risk vs. Reward Tradeoff: Risk management allows investors to strike a balance between risk and reward. Every investment carries a certain degree of risk, but effective risk management helps determine the acceptable level of risk for potential returns. By understanding and managing risk, investors can optimize their portfolio performance while avoiding excessive exposure to potential losses.

3. Emotion Control: Investing can be an emotionally charged activity, and emotions like fear and greed can cloud judgment. Risk management strategies provide a disciplined approach to decision-making, helping investors avoid impulsive or emotionally driven investment decisions. By adhering to predetermined

risk management rules, investors can make more rational and objective choices.

4. Diversification: Risk management involves diversifying investments across different asset classes, sectors, and geographies. Diversification helps spread risk and reduces the impact of any single investment on the overall portfolio. A well-diversified portfolio can mitigate the potential damage caused by the poor performance of individual investments.

5. Stress Testing: Risk management involves stress testing portfolios to assess their resilience in adverse market conditions. By simulating different market scenarios, investors can evaluate the potential impact on their investments and make necessary adjustments. Stress testing helps identify vulnerabilities and refine the investment strategy accordingly.

6. Consistency and Long-Term Success: Risk management promotes consistency in investment performance. By implementing a systematic and disciplined approach, investors can avoid big losses and minimize the impact of market downturns. Consistent risk management over the long term enhances the probability of achieving investment goals and generating sustainable returns.

7. Risk Awareness: Risk management fosters a deeper understanding of the risks associated with investments. It encourages investors to assess and quantify risks, identify potential vulnerabilities, and develop contingency plans. Being aware of the risks involved allows for more informed decision-making and proactive risk mitigation.

8. Adaptation to Changing Market Conditions: Risk management enables investors to adapt to changing market conditions. By regularly monitoring and evaluating risks, investors can adjust their strategies to

align with evolving market dynamics. Flexibility and the ability to adapt to new risks are essential for navigating uncertain and volatile markets.

In summary, risk management is essential for preserving capital, optimizing risk-reward tradeoffs, maintaining emotional control, diversifying investments, stress testing portfolios, achieving consistency, enhancing long-term success, promoting risk awareness, and adapting to changing market conditions. Implementing effective risk management strategies can significantly improve the likelihood of investment success and help investors navigate the inherent uncertainties of financial markets.

5.2 Assessing Risk Tolerance

Assessing risk tolerance is an important step in financial planning and investment decision-making. Risk tolerance refers to an individual's ability to endure and handle potential losses or fluctuations in investment returns. It helps determine the level of risk that an individual or investor is comfortable taking on in pursuit of their financial goals. Here's an overview of assessing risk tolerance:

1. Financial Goals: Start by understanding your financial goals, both short-term and long-term. Consider factors such as the time horizon for achieving these goals, the specific objectives (e.g., retirement, buying a house, funding education), and the level of flexibility or urgency associated with each goal.

2. Risk Capacity: Assess your financial capacity to take on risk. This involves evaluating your current financial situation, including income, expenses, assets, liabilities, and liquidity. Consider factors such as your income stability, savings, emergency fund, and the ability to absorb potential losses without compromising your financial well-being.

3. Time Horizon: Evaluate your investment time horizon, which is the length of time you plan to invest before needing to access the funds. Longer time horizons generally allow for a higher tolerance for risk, as there is more opportunity to recover from market downturns or fluctuations.

4. Investment Knowledge and Experience: Consider your knowledge and experience in investing. Investors with a greater understanding of financial markets and investment products may have a higher risk tolerance as they feel more confident in managing potential risks.

5. Personal Preferences and Comfort Level: Assess your personal comfort level with risk. Some individuals may have a natural inclination to take on more risk, while others may prefer more conservative approaches. Consider your attitudes toward risk, your ability to handle market volatility, and your emotional reactions to investment losses or gains.

6. Risk Tolerance Questionnaires: Utilize risk tolerance questionnaires or tools provided by financial advisors or investment platforms. These questionnaires typically ask a series of questions about your financial situation, investment knowledge, and attitudes toward risk. The answers help determine an appropriate risk tolerance level and asset allocation strategy.

7. Considerations for Risk Aversion: Take into account any factors that may make you more risk-averse, such as a low tolerance for uncertainty or anxiety about potential losses. Some individuals may prioritize capital preservation over higher returns and be more comfortable with lower-risk investment options.

8. Regular Reassessment: Remember that risk tolerance can change over time. Life circumstances, financial goals, and personal factors may evolve, leading to

a reassessment of risk tolerance. It's important to periodically review and adjust your risk tolerance as needed.

Understanding your risk tolerance is crucial for constructing an investment portfolio that aligns with your financial goals, time horizon, and personal comfort level. It helps strike a balance between risk and potential returns, ensuring that you can stay committed to your investment strategy even during periods of market volatility. It is recommended to seek the guidance of a financial advisor who can assist in the assessment of your risk tolerance and provide appropriate investment recommendations based on your individual circumstances.

5.3 Setting Stop-Loss Orders

Setting stop-loss orders is a risk management technique used by investors and traders to limit potential losses on their investments. A stop-loss order is an instruction given to a broker or trading platform to automatically sell a security if its price reaches a specified level. It is designed to protect investors from significant downside risk and help preserve capital. Here's an overview of setting stop-loss orders:

1. Risk Management: The primary purpose of setting stop-loss orders is to manage risk. By defining a predetermined price level at which to exit a position, investors can limit their potential losses if the market moves against them. This allows for greater control over risk exposure and prevents emotions from driving impulsive decisions during volatile market conditions.

2. Determining the Stop-Loss Level: The stop-loss level is the price level at which an investor is willing to exit a position. It is typically set below the current market price for long positions and above the market price for short positions. The specific stop-loss level will vary based on individual risk tolerance, investment strategy,

and the volatility of the security being traded.

3. Technical Analysis: Stop-loss levels can be determined using technical analysis techniques. Traders often set stop-loss orders at key support or resistance levels, trendlines, moving averages, or other technical indicators. The aim is to place the stop-loss level at a point that suggests a potential reversal or significant change in the market trend.

4. Volatility Considerations: The level of volatility in the market and the specific security being traded should be considered when setting stop-loss orders. Highly volatile securities may require wider stop-loss levels to account for price fluctuations, while less volatile securities may have tighter stop-loss levels.

5. Adjusting Stop-Loss Levels: Stop-loss levels should be periodically reviewed and adjusted as market conditions change. If the price of the security moves in a favorable direction, the stop-loss level can be adjusted higher (for long positions) or lower (for short positions) to lock in profits and protect against potential reversals.

6. Psychological Factors: Setting stop-loss orders helps overcome emotional biases and prevents investors from holding on to losing positions for too long. It enforces discipline in adhering to predetermined risk management strategies and reduces the impact of emotional decision-making.

7. Market Liquidity: When setting stop-loss orders, it is important to consider the liquidity of the security. In illiquid markets, the execution of stop-loss orders may be more challenging, leading to potential slippage in the order execution price. This is particularly relevant for large positions or during periods of heightened market volatility.

8. Monitoring and Execution: Once a stop-loss order is

set, it is essential to monitor the market and the performance of the security. If the stop-loss level is triggered, the order is executed automatically, resulting in the sale of the position at the prevailing market price. It is important to ensure that the trading platform or broker offers reliable execution of stop-loss orders.

Setting stop-loss orders is a proactive risk management strategy that helps investors limit potential losses and protect their capital. By defining predetermined exit points, investors can mitigate the impact of adverse market movements and maintain discipline in their investment approach. However, it is important to note that stop-loss orders do not guarantee the specified price execution, especially in fast-moving markets or during market gaps. Therefore, careful consideration should be given to the selection of appropriate stop-loss levels and the monitoring of market conditions.

5.4 Position Sizing Strategies

Position sizing strategies refer to the techniques used by investors and traders to determine the appropriate size or allocation of capital to be allocated to each investment or trading position. Position sizing is a critical aspect of risk management and portfolio optimization. It helps investors optimize returns while managing risk and ensuring capital preservation. Here's an overview of some common position sizing strategies:

1. Fixed Dollar Amount: In this strategy, a fixed amount of capital is allocated to each position. For example, an investor may decide to allocate $10,000 to each trade or investment. The position size remains the same regardless of the price or volatility of the security. This strategy is simple to implement but does not take into account the individual risk profile of each investment.

2. Fixed Percentage of Portfolio: With this approach, a fixed percentage of the total portfolio value is allocated

to each position. For instance, an investor may decide to allocate 5% of their portfolio to each trade. As the portfolio value fluctuates, the position size adjusts accordingly. This strategy helps maintain a consistent risk level across different investments but may result in larger positions in more volatile securities.

3. Risk-Based Position Sizing: This strategy considers the level of risk associated with each investment or trade. It involves determining the maximum acceptable risk or loss for each position and calculating the position size based on that risk tolerance. This can be achieved by setting a specific dollar amount or percentage of capital at risk for each trade. For example, an investor may decide to risk a maximum of 2% of their portfolio value on any given trade. The position size is then calculated based on the desired risk level and the stop-loss level.

4. Volatility-Based Position Sizing: This approach adjusts the position size based on the volatility of the security being traded. More volatile securities may require smaller position sizes to account for the higher potential price swings. A common method to calculate position size based on volatility is the "Volatility Quotient" or "Volatility Adjusted Position Size" formula, which incorporates measures such as average true range (ATR) or standard deviation.

5. Kelly Criterion: The Kelly Criterion is a mathematical formula used to determine the optimal position size based on the expected return and probability of success of each trade. It considers the potential reward-to-risk ratio and provides a position size recommendation that maximizes the long-term growth of capital. The formula takes into account the investor's win rate (percentage of winning trades) and the average size of winning and losing trades.

6. Factor-Based Position Sizing: In this approach, position sizes are determined based on specific factors or indicators. For example, an investor may allocate larger positions to securities that meet certain fundamental criteria or technical indicators, such as strong earnings growth, low price-to-earnings ratio, or bullish chart patterns. The position size is adjusted based on the presence or absence of these factors.

It's important to note that position sizing strategies should be tailored to individual risk tolerance, investment goals, and trading style. Risk management should always be a primary consideration when determining position sizes. Investors should also consider the liquidity of the security, the overall diversification of the portfolio, and any regulatory or margin requirements that may impact position sizing decisions.

By implementing appropriate position sizing strategies, investors can manage risk, optimize returns, and maintain consistency in their investment approach. However, it's crucial to regularly review and adjust position sizes based on changes in market conditions, portfolio performance, and individual risk preferences.

5.5 Diversification and Portfolio Allocation

Diversification and portfolio allocation are important concepts in investment management that help investors manage risk and optimize returns by spreading their investments across different assets or asset classes. Here's an overview of these topics:

1. Diversification: Diversification involves investing in a variety of assets to reduce the impact of any single investment on the overall portfolio. The goal is to create a portfolio that is less susceptible to the risks associated with individual investments or market fluctuations. Diversification can be achieved through various means:

   a. Asset Allocation: Diversify the portfolio across

different asset classes such as stocks, bonds, cash, real estate, and commodities. Each asset class has different risk-return characteristics, so combining them can help balance the overall risk exposure.

b. Sector Allocation: Allocate investments across different sectors or industries. By investing in companies from various sectors, investors can reduce the impact of sector-specific risks and benefit from the performance of different sectors.

c. Geographic Diversification: Spread investments across different countries and regions. This helps mitigate country-specific risks, political instability, economic fluctuations, and currency risks.

d. Company Size: Diversify holdings across companies of different sizes, such as large-cap, mid-cap, and small-cap stocks. Each category has distinct risk profiles and growth potential, and diversifying across them can help balance the portfolio's risk-return characteristics.

e. Investment Instruments: Diversify across different investment instruments, including stocks, bonds, mutual funds, exchange-traded funds (ETFs), derivatives, and alternative investments. This helps reduce exposure to any single investment type.

The purpose of diversification is to reduce the potential impact of negative events on the overall portfolio while still participating in the potential returns of different investments. However, diversification does not guarantee profits or eliminate all risks, including the risk of loss.

2. Portfolio Allocation: Portfolio allocation involves determining the optimal mix of different asset classes or investments within a portfolio based on an individual's investment goals, risk tolerance, time horizon, and market conditions. It aims to strike a balance between risk and return.

a. Risk Appetite: Investors with a higher risk appetite may allocate a larger portion of their portfolio to riskier assets, such as stocks or alternative investments, in pursuit of higher returns. Conversely, more risk-averse investors may allocate a larger portion to fewer volatile assets, such as bonds or cash.

b. Time Horizon: The time horizon for investment is an important consideration in portfolio allocation. Longer investment horizons may allow for a higher allocation to growth-oriented assets like stocks, while shorter horizons may warrant a greater allocation to more stable assets like bonds or cash.

c. Investment Goals: The specific goals of an investor, such as retirement planning, funding education, or buying a house, influence the portfolio allocation. Different goals may require different risk-return profiles, and the allocation should align with the desired outcomes.

d. Rebalancing: Regular portfolio rebalancing is necessary to maintain the desired asset allocation. As market conditions change and certain investments outperform or underperform, the portfolio may deviate from the target allocation. Rebalancing involves buying or selling assets to bring the portfolio back to the desired allocation.

e. Risk-Return Tradeoff: Portfolio allocation seeks to strike a balance between the desired level of return and the acceptable level of risk. Investors should assess their risk tolerance and consider the potential risks associated with different asset classes or investments when determining the allocation.

Proper portfolio allocation helps manage risk by spreading investments across different assets with varying risk profiles. It also allows investors to benefit from the potential returns of different asset classes and diversify against specific risks associated with individual investments.

It's important to note that diversification and portfolio allocation strategies should be tailored to individual circumstances, investment goals, and risk tolerance. There is no one-size-fits-all approach, and it's advisable to seek professional advice or conduct thorough research before making investment decisions. Regular monitoring and periodic adjustments to the portfolio allocation may be necessary to ensure it remains aligned with changing market conditions and personal goals.

CHAPTER 6: TRADING STRATEGIES AND TECHNIQUES

6.1 Order Types and Execution

Order types and execution are key aspects of trading in financial markets. They involve the various types of orders that investors can place to buy or sell securities and the process by which these orders are executed. Here's an overview of order types and execution:

1. Market Orders: A market order is the simplest and most common type of order. When placing a market order, investors instruct their broker to execute the order immediately at the prevailing market price. The order is executed as quickly as possible, and the investor buys or sells the security at the best available price in the market. Market orders provide certainty of execution but do not guarantee a specific price.

2. Limit Orders: A limit order allows investors to specify the maximum price they are willing to pay to buy or the minimum price they are willing to accept to sell a security. For a buy limit order, the order is executed at or below the specified price. For a sell limit order, the order is executed at or above the specified price. Limit orders provide price control but may not be executed if the specified price is not reached.

3. Stop Orders: Stop orders, also known as stop-loss orders or stop-limit orders, are used to limit potential losses or protect profits. A stop order becomes a market order when the specified price, known as the stop price, is reached. For a stop-loss order, the order is triggered to sell a security if the price falls to or below the stop price.

For a stop-limit order, the order becomes a limit order to sell at the specified limit price once the stop price is reached. Stop orders help manage risk but are not guaranteed to be executed at the specified price.

4. Stop-Limit Orders: Stop-limit orders combine elements of stop orders and limit orders. They have a stop price and a limit price. When the stop price is reached, the order becomes a limit order with the specified limit price. The order is executed at or better than the limit price, but there is no guarantee of execution.

5. Market-on-Close (MOC) and Limit-on-Close (LOC) Orders: These order types are used to execute trades at the closing price of the trading day. MOC orders are executed at the market price, while LOC orders are executed at or better than the specified limit price.

6. Immediate-or-Cancel (IOC) Orders: IOC orders require immediate execution of any portion of the order that can be filled, and the remaining unfilled portion is canceled. IOC orders prioritize immediate execution over partial fills.

7. Fill-or-Kill (FOK) Orders: FOK orders require the complete execution of the entire order quantity at the specified price or better. If the entire order cannot be filled immediately, it is canceled.

8. Good-Til-Canceled (GTC) Orders: GTC orders remain active until they are executed or canceled by the investor. They do not expire at the end of the trading day and remain in the order book until executed or manually canceled.

Order execution is the process by which brokerage firms or exchanges fulfill investor orders. The execution depends on factors such as the order type, market conditions, liquidity, and trading rules. In liquid markets, orders are usually executed quickly and at or close to the desired price. However, in volatile or illiquid markets, there may be delays or price discrepancies between the requested and executed prices.

It's important for investors to understand the different order types, their advantages, and limitations. Consideration should be given to factors such as price control, speed of execution, risk management, and the specific requirements of the investment strategy. Consulting with a broker or financial advisor can help determine the most appropriate order type for specific trading needs.

6.2 Trade Entry Techniques

Trade entry techniques refer to the strategies and methods used by traders to enter positions in financial markets. These techniques help traders identify optimal entry points based on their trading strategy, market analysis, and risk management considerations. Here's an overview of some common trade entry techniques:

1. Breakout Trading: Breakout trading involves entering a trade when the price of a security breaks out of a defined price range or a key technical level. Traders look for breakouts above resistance levels or below support levels, anticipating that the price will continue to move in the direction of the breakout.

2. Pullback Trading: Pullback trading involves entering a trade after a temporary retracement or pullback in the price of a security. Traders identify a strong trend and wait for a temporary price decline before entering a position in the direction of the overall trend. This technique aims to capture the resumption of the trend after a brief consolidation.

3. Trend-following: Trend-following strategies involve entering trades in the direction of a well-established trend. Traders identify a trending market using technical indicators, chart patterns, or trendlines.

They enter positions when the price confirms the continuation of the trend, such as a higher high in an uptrend or a lower low in a downtrend.

4. Reversal Trading: Reversal trading involves entering trades when a market or security shows signs of a trend reversal. Traders look for signals that indicate a potential change in the direction of the price movement, such as the formation of chart patterns (e.g., double tops or bottoms) or divergences in technical indicators. Reversal traders aim to capture the early stages of a new trend.

5. Candlestick Patterns: Candlestick patterns provide visual cues about market sentiment and potential reversals. Traders use specific candlestick patterns, such as doji, engulfing patterns, or hammer patterns, to identify entry opportunities. These patterns suggest a shift in buying or selling pressure and can be used to time trade entries.

6. News Trading: News trading involves entering trades based on significant news events or economic data releases. Traders aim to capture price movements resulting from market reactions to news. They may enter positions before the news release, anticipating the impact, or react quickly to news-driven price movements.

7. Indicator-based Strategies: Traders use technical indicators, such as moving averages, oscillators (e.g., RSI, MACD), or stochastic indicators, to generate entry signals. These indicators provide insights into price momentum, overbought or oversold conditions, or trend strength. Traders enter positions based on the signals generated by these indicators.

8. Fundamental Analysis: Fundamental analysis involves analyzing the underlying financial and economic factors

that can impact the price of a security. Traders using fundamental analysis may enter positions based on their assessment of a company's financial health, industry trends, or macroeconomic factors.

It's important to note that trade entry techniques should align with an individual's trading style, risk tolerance, and the specific market conditions. Traders often use a combination of techniques or customize them based on their preferences. Risk management and the use of stop-loss orders are crucial when entering trades to limit potential losses and protect capital. Traders should also consider the availability of liquidity, slippage risks, and transaction costs when executing trade entries.

6.3 Trade Exit Strategies

Trade exit strategies refer to the techniques and approaches used by traders to close or exit their positions in financial markets. These strategies are crucial for managing risk, maximizing profits, and preserving capital. A well-defined and disciplined trade exit strategy helps traders make informed decisions about when to exit a trade. Here's an overview of some common trade exit strategies:

1. Profit Target: Profit target is a predetermined price level at which a trader plans to exit a position to lock in profits. The profit target can be based on technical analysis indicators, chart patterns, or predetermined price levels. By setting a profit target, traders aim to capture a specific amount of profit and avoid getting greedy or waiting for excessive gains that may not materialize.

2. Stop-Loss Orders: Stop-loss orders are used to exit a trade when the price reaches a predefined level to limit potential losses. It is a risk management tool that helps protect against significant adverse market moves. Traders set stop-loss levels based on their risk

tolerance, the volatility of the security, and technical analysis indicators. Stop-loss orders ensure that losses are controlled and allow traders to move on to the next opportunity.

3. Trailing Stop: A trailing stop is an order type that adjusts the stop-loss level as the price moves in favor of the trade. It is designed to protect profits by maintaining a dynamic stop-loss level. If the price moves in the desired direction, the trailing stop automatically adjusts to lock in profits. However, if the price reverses, the trailing stop will be triggered, and the trade will be exited.

4. Time-Based Exit: Traders may choose to exit a trade based on a predetermined time frame. For example, they may decide to close a trade at the end of the trading day or before an important news event that could impact the market. Time-based exits help traders avoid potential market volatility or overnight risks and allow them to reassess market conditions.

5. Break-Even Stop: A break-even stop is a technique where the stop-loss level is adjusted to the entry price once the trade has moved in the trader's favor. By moving the stop-loss level to the entry price, traders ensure that they will not incur a loss even if the trade reverses. This strategy helps protect capital and eliminates the risk of losing on a winning trade.

6. Trailing Profit Target: Similar to a trailing stop, a trailing profit target adjusts the take-profit level as the price moves in the trader's favor. It allows traders to capture additional profits if the price continues to trend in the desired direction. The trailing profit target is adjusted based on predefined rules or technical indicators.

7. Technical Analysis Signals: Traders may choose to exit a trade based on specific technical analysis signals. These signals can include the crossing of moving averages,

trendline breaks, or the occurrence of specific chart patterns. By following these signals, traders aim to capture potential trend reversals or signs of weakening momentum.

8. Fundamental Factors: Fundamental analysis can also guide trade exit decisions. Traders may choose to exit a trade based on changes in company fundamentals, economic data releases, or shifts in market sentiment. By considering fundamental factors, traders aim to align their trade exits with the underlying changes in the market.

It's important to note that trade exit strategies should be based on a trader's individual trading style, risk tolerance, and market conditions. Traders should have clear and predefined criteria for exiting a trade to avoid emotional decision-making and to ensure consistency in their approach. Risk management, including the use of stop-loss orders, is essential to protect against potential losses. Regular monitoring of trades and adjustments to exit strategies may be necessary based on changing market conditions.

6.4 Managing Trades and Adjusting Stops

Managing trades and adjusting stops is a crucial aspect of active trading. Once a trade is initiated, managing it effectively involves monitoring its progress, making necessary adjustments, and actively managing risk. Here's an overview of managing trades and adjusting stops:

1. Monitoring Trade Progress: Traders need to regularly monitor the progress of their trades to assess whether they are moving in the desired direction. This involves tracking the price movement, analyzing relevant technical indicators or chart patterns, and staying updated on market news and events that may impact the trade.

2. Trailing Stop Adjustments: Trailing stops are an effective way to protect profits and limit potential losses as a trade move in the trader's favor. Adjusting the trailing stop involves periodically updating the stop-loss level to lock in profits or protect a larger portion of the gains. Traders can use various methods for trailing stop adjustments, such as percentage-based trailing stops or based on specific technical indicators or support/resistance levels.

3. Stop-Loss Orders: Traders should regularly reassess their initial stop-loss orders to ensure they are still appropriate based on the evolving market conditions and trade dynamics. If necessary, stop-loss orders can be tightened to minimize potential losses or adjusted to give the trade more room to breathe based on increased volatility or changed market conditions.

4. Profit Targets: Traders should review their profit targets periodically and adjust them if necessary. If the trade is moving strongly in the desired direction, traders may choose to adjust the profit target higher to capture additional gains. On the other hand, if the trade is showing signs of weakness or reaching a significant resistance level, traders may consider taking profits earlier.

5. Risk-Reward Ratio Assessment: Continuously assessing the risk-reward ratio of a trade is important. If the potential reward decreases or the risk increases due to changing market conditions, traders may decide to exit the trade or adjust their stop-loss levels accordingly. This ensures that the trade remains aligned with the desired risk-reward profile.

6. News and Event Management: Traders should stay aware of upcoming news releases or events that may impact their trades. Particularly significant news

events can cause rapid price movements and increased volatility. Traders may choose to adjust their stop-loss levels or exit trades before such events to manage potential risks.

7. Trade Documentation: Keeping detailed records of trades is essential for effective trade management. This includes documenting the entry and exit points, stop-loss levels, profit targets, and reasons for initiating the trade. These records provide insights into the effectiveness of trade management strategies and help traders learn from their experiences.

8. Emotional Discipline: Managing trades and adjusting stops requires emotional discipline. It's important to stick to the predefined trading plan and avoid making impulsive decisions based on fear or greed. Emotion-driven decisions can lead to inconsistent or ineffective trade management.

Regularly assessing trade progress, adjusting stops, and managing risk are critical for successful trading. Traders should remain flexible and adapt their trade management strategies based on changing market conditions, new information, and evolving trade dynamics. Effective trade management helps maximize profits, minimize losses, and maintain a disciplined approach to trading.

6.5 Trading Psychology and Emotional Discipline

Trading psychology and emotional discipline play a crucial role in the success of traders. Trading can be a highly emotional and psychologically demanding endeavor, and the ability to manage emotions and maintain discipline is essential for making rational and objective trading decisions. Here's an overview of trading psychology and emotional discipline:

1. Emotions in Trading: Emotions such as fear, greed, excitement, and frustration can significantly impact

trading decisions. Fear can lead to missed opportunities or premature exits, while greed can result in excessive risk-taking. Emotional reactions to gains or losses can cloud judgment and lead to impulsive or irrational decisions.

2. Self-Awareness: Successful traders cultivate self-awareness by understanding their emotions, biases, and triggers that may affect their decision-making. By recognizing their emotional states, traders can take steps to manage and control their emotions, making more rational trading decisions.

3. Emotional Discipline: Emotional discipline involves maintaining control over emotions and adhering to a well-defined trading plan and strategy. Traders with emotional discipline are less likely to make impulsive trades, chase after losses, or deviate from their predetermined risk management rules.

4. Risk Management: Emotional discipline is closely tied to risk management. Traders with emotional discipline are more likely to stick to their risk management strategies, such as setting appropriate stop-loss levels and position sizes, and avoiding excessive risk-taking. They prioritize capital preservation over the allure of potential gains.

5. Patience and Impulse Control: Patience is a key attribute of successful traders. Impulse control allows traders to resist the urge to act on short-term market fluctuations or succumb to the fear of missing out (FOMO). Patient traders wait for high-probability setups and avoid trading on emotions or random market noise.

6. Developing a Trading Plan: Having a well-defined trading plan helps foster emotional discipline. A trading plan outlines specific entry and exit criteria, risk management strategies, and guidelines for trade execution. By following a trading plan, traders can

minimize emotional decision-making and rely on a systematic approach.

7. Continuous Learning and Adaptation: Successful traders understand that trading is an ongoing learning process. They continually seek to improve their knowledge, skills, and strategies. This willingness to learn and adapt helps traders maintain emotional discipline by being open to new information and adjusting their approaches based on market conditions.

8. Psychological Resilience: Trading involves dealing with uncertainties, losses, and setbacks. Psychological resilience enables traders to bounce back from losses or mistakes and maintain a positive mindset. Resilient traders view losses as learning experiences rather than personal failures and maintain a long-term perspective.

9. Mindfulness and Emotional Regulation Techniques: Practices such as mindfulness, meditation, deep breathing exercises, and visualization can help traders manage stress, increase self-awareness, and regulate emotions. These techniques can be beneficial in maintaining emotional discipline and clarity during the trading process.

10. Emotional Support: Traders may benefit from seeking emotional support from mentors, fellow traders, or support groups. Sharing experiences, discussing challenges, and receiving guidance can help traders manage their emotions and stay focused on their trading goals.

Trading psychology and emotional discipline are critical components of successful trading. By understanding and managing their emotions, developing a well-defined trading plan, practicing risk management, and continuously learning and adapting, traders can improve their decision-making and increase their chances of long-term success in the financial markets.

CHAPTER 7: ADVANCED TRADING CONCEPTS

7.1 Swing Trading

Swing trading is a trading strategy that aims to capture short to medium-term price swings or "swings" in financial markets. Swing traders seek to profit from the price fluctuations that occur within an established trend, whether it's an uptrend or a downtrend. Unlike day traders who typically close their positions within a single trading day, swing traders hold their positions for a few days to several weeks, taking advantage of intermediate-term price movements. Here's an overview of swing trading:

1. Timeframe: Swing trading operates in a timeframe between day trading and long-term investing. It focuses on capturing shorter-term price movements within the context of the overall trend.

2. Trend Identification: Swing traders aim to identify and trade within the prevailing trend. They use technical analysis tools, such as trendlines, moving averages, and chart patterns, to determine the direction of the trend.

3. Entry Points: Swing traders look for entry points that provide favorable risk-reward ratios. They typically enter a trade when they believe the price has completed a corrective move within the larger trend and is likely to resume its primary direction. Entry points can be identified through technical indicators, chart patterns (such as breakouts or pullbacks), or a combination of factors.

4. Position Management: Swing traders actively manage their positions by monitoring the market and adjusting their stop-loss orders and profit targets. They aim to

protect profits by trailing stop-loss orders to lock in gains as the price moves in their favor. They may also adjust their profit targets if the price shows strong momentum.

5. Risk Management: Effective risk management is essential in swing trading. Swing traders determine their risk tolerance and set appropriate stop-loss orders to limit potential losses. Risk-reward ratios are carefully considered to ensure that potential profits outweigh potential losses.

6. Fundamental Analysis: While swing trading primarily relies on technical analysis, some swing traders may also consider fundamental factors, such as news events or company-specific developments, that can impact the price movement of the security they are trading.

7. Trade Frequency: Swing trading typically involves fewer trades compared to day trading. Swing traders focus on high-probability setups and select their trades more selectively, as they aim to capture larger price moves over a relatively short period.

8. Market Selection: Swing traders can apply their strategy to various financial markets, including stocks, futures, currencies, and commodities. They choose markets with sufficient liquidity and volatility to allow for significant price swings.

9. Discipline and Patience: Successful swing trading requires discipline and patience. Swing traders must adhere to their predefined trading plan, follow their entry and exit rules, and avoid impulsive trading decisions based on emotions or short-term market fluctuations.

10. Trade Exit: Swing traders exit their trades when the price reaches their profit targets or if the market conditions invalidate their initial trade setup. They may

also exit trades if the price shows signs of reversing against their position or if the trend they identified begins to weaken.

Swing trading offers opportunities for traders to capture shorter-term price movements while avoiding the need for constant monitoring associated with day trading. It requires a good understanding of technical analysis, risk management, and the ability to adapt to changing market conditions. Like any trading strategy, swing trading carries risks, and traders should carefully consider their risk tolerance and have a well-defined trading plan before engaging in swing trading activities.

7.2 Day Trading

Day trading is a trading strategy where traders aim to profit from short-term price movements in financial markets by entering and exiting trades within the same trading day. Day traders actively monitor the markets throughout the day and capitalize on intraday price fluctuations. Here's an overview of day trading:

1. Timeframe: Day trading operates within the timeframe of a single trading day. Day traders do not hold positions overnight, which means they are not exposed to the risks associated with overnight market movements or news events.

2. High Trading Frequency: Day traders execute a relatively high number of trades within a single trading session. They take advantage of small price movements and aim to accumulate profits over multiple trades rather than relying on large gains from a single trade.

3. Short-Term Strategies: Day traders employ various short-term trading strategies, such as scalping, momentum trading, or fading. Scalping involves quickly entering and exiting trades to capture small price movements, while momentum trading involves following the direction of strong price trends. Fading

involves taking contrarian positions against prevailing market trends.

4. Technical Analysis: Day traders primarily rely on technical analysis tools and indicators to identify trading opportunities. They analyze price charts, patterns, support and resistance levels, and indicators like moving averages, oscillators, and volume to make their trading decisions.

5. Volatility and Liquidity: Day traders prefer markets or securities with high liquidity and volatility. High liquidity ensures that there are enough buyers and sellers to execute trades quickly, while volatility creates price movements that provide trading opportunities.

6. Risk Management: Effective risk management is crucial in day trading. Day traders set strict stop-loss orders to limit potential losses and use position sizing techniques to control risk. They also consider the risk-reward ratio before entering a trade to ensure potential profits justify the risk taken.

7. Speed and Technology: Day traders rely on fast execution platforms and real-time market data to react quickly to changing market conditions. They require robust internet connections, direct market access (DMA), and sophisticated trading software to enter and exit trades swiftly.

8. Emotional Discipline: Day trading can be emotionally demanding due to the fast-paced nature of the activity and the potential for rapid gains or losses. Emotional discipline is critical to sticking to a trading plan, managing risk, and avoiding impulsive decisions based on emotions or market noise.

9. Continuous Learning and Adaptation: Day traders constantly learn and adapt to changing market conditions. They review their trading strategies,

evaluate their trades, and analyze their performance to identify strengths and weaknesses. Continuous learning helps them refine their strategies and improve their decision-making over time.

10. Regulatory Considerations: Day traders should be aware of the regulatory requirements and restrictions related to day trading, such as pattern day trading rules or margin requirements imposed by regulatory bodies in their jurisdiction.

Day trading requires dedicated time, effort, and knowledge. It is a high-risk activity that can be rewarding but also challenging. Traders considering day trading should thoroughly understand the risks involved, develop a well-defined trading plan, practice proper risk management, and consider seeking professional advice or education before engaging in day trading activities.

7.3 Options Trading

Options trading is a type of derivative trading that involves the buying and selling of options contracts based on underlying assets such as stocks, indices, commodities, or currencies. Options provide traders with the right, but not the obligation, to buy or sell the underlying asset at a predetermined price (known as the strike price) within a specified period (known as the expiration date). Here's an overview of options trading:

1. Call and Put Options: There are two types of options: call options and put options. A call option gives the holder the right to buy the underlying asset at the strike price before the expiration date. A put option gives the holder the right to sell the underlying asset at the strike price before the expiration date.

2. Options Premium: The price of an options contract is known as the premium. The premium is influenced by factors such as the current price of the underlying asset, the strike price, time remaining until expiration,

implied volatility, and interest rates.

3. Buying Options: Traders can buy options contracts to speculate on the price movement of the underlying asset. If they believe the price will rise, they can buy call options. If they anticipate a price decline, they can buy put options. The potential profit is unlimited for buying options, but the risk is limited to the premium paid.

4. Selling Options: Traders can also sell options contracts to generate income. When selling options, traders take on the obligation to buy (in the case of selling put options) or sell (in the case of selling call options) the underlying asset if the option buyer exercises their right. Selling options generates a premium, but the potential risk is significant, as losses can be substantial if the market moves against the trader.

5. Option Strategies: Traders can use various option strategies to achieve different objectives. Common strategies include buying or selling single options, as well as more complex strategies like covered calls, protective puts, straddles, strangles, spreads, and combinations. These strategies involve combining multiple options contracts to manage risk, hedge positions, or capitalize on specific market conditions.

6. Options Expiration: Options have a finite lifespan, and they expire on a specific date. Traders can choose options with different expiration dates, ranging from days to months. Once an option expires, it becomes worthless, and the trader loses the premium paid.

7. Options Pricing and Greeks: Options pricing is influenced by factors known as "Greeks." These include delta, gamma, theta, vega, and rho. Greeks help traders assess the sensitivity of options prices to changes in the underlying asset price, volatility, time decay, and other factors. Understanding the Greeks is important for

managing options positions and assessing risk.

8. Risk Management: Options trading involves risks, including the potential loss of the premium paid. Traders should carefully assess their risk tolerance, understand the potential outcomes of their options positions, and use appropriate risk management strategies such as stop-loss orders, position sizing, and portfolio diversification.

9. Regulatory Considerations: Options trading is subject to regulations and requirements imposed by regulatory bodies. Traders should be aware of the specific regulations in their jurisdiction, such as margin requirements, pattern day trading rules, or disclosure obligations.

Options trading provides flexibility and the opportunity to profit from price movements in various markets. However, it also carries significant risks due to the complex nature of options and the potential for substantial losses. Traders interested in options trading should acquire a solid understanding of options concepts, strategies, and risk management techniques, and consider seeking professional guidance or education before engaging in options trading activities.

7.4 Algorithmic Trading

Algorithmic trading, also known as algo trading or automated trading, refers to the use of computer programs or algorithms to execute trading strategies in financial markets. These algorithms are designed to analyze market data, identify trading opportunities, and automatically place trades based on predefined rules and parameters. Here's an overview of algorithmic trading:

1. Predefined Trading Rules: Algorithmic trading relies on a set of predefined rules and parameters that dictate

when and how trades should be executed. These rules can be based on technical indicators, mathematical models, statistical analysis, or a combination of factors. The algorithms are programmed to follow these rules precisely without human intervention.

2. Market Data Analysis: Algorithmic trading algorithms analyze large volumes of market data, including price feeds, order book data, news, and other relevant information. They use this data to identify patterns, trends, and trading opportunities that may not be easily detectable by human traders. The algorithms can process data and make trading decisions at high speeds, often in milliseconds.

3. Order Placement and Execution: Once a trading opportunity is identified, the algorithm automatically generates and places orders in the market. It can execute trades across various financial instruments, including stocks, futures, options, currencies, and commodities. Algorithms can split large orders into smaller ones to minimize market impact and improve execution prices. Trades are typically executed electronically, connecting to exchanges or other trading venues.

4. Efficiency and Speed: Algorithmic trading is known for its speed and efficiency. Computers can analyze market data and execute trades much faster than human traders. This enables algorithmic traders to take advantage of fleeting opportunities, exploit small price discrepancies, and react swiftly to market conditions.

5. High-Frequency Trading (HFT): High-frequency trading is a subset of algorithmic trading characterized by extremely high trading volumes and low holding periods. HFT algorithms aim to profit from small price discrepancies that exist for very brief periods, often in microseconds. HFT strategies rely on sophisticated

technology, low-latency infrastructure, and co-location services to achieve ultra-fast execution speeds.

6. Back testing and Optimization: Before deploying algorithms in live trading, they are often back tested and optimized using historical market data. Back testing involves running the algorithm on past market data to assess its performance and profitability. Optimization involves adjusting the algorithm's parameters to improve its performance based on historical results. These processes help refine the algorithm and fine-tune its trading rules.

7. Risk Management: Algorithmic trading incorporates risk management techniques to control potential losses. Risk management rules, such as stop-loss orders or position-sizing algorithms, are built into the trading algorithms to limit exposure and protect capital. Risk controls are implemented to prevent excessive risk-taking or unexpected market events.

8. Regulatory Considerations: Algorithmic trading is subject to regulatory oversight in many jurisdictions. Regulations may include requirements related to algorithmic trading strategies, risk controls, order types, market manipulation prevention, and reporting obligations. Traders involved in algorithmic trading should be familiar with the regulatory framework applicable in their region.

Algorithmic trading has become prevalent in modern financial markets, with institutional investors, hedge funds, and proprietary trading firms being active participants. The use of algorithms enables increased trading efficiency, liquidity provision, and the ability to implement complex strategies. However, algorithmic trading also presents risks, such as technology failures, connectivity issues, and the potential for unintended consequences. Understanding the intricacies of algorithmic trading and having robust risk management controls are essential for successful implementation.

7.5 Position Trading

Position trading is a long-term trading strategy that focuses on capturing larger price movements in financial markets. Unlike day trading or swing trading, which aim to capitalize on short-term price fluctuations, position trading involves holding positions for an extended period, often lasting weeks, months, or even years. Here's an overview of position trading:

1. Long-Term Perspective: Position traders take a long-term view of the market and aim to profit from major trends or price movements in the underlying asset. They are not concerned with short-term price fluctuations or intraday volatility.

2. Fundamental Analysis: Position trading often relies heavily on fundamental analysis to identify potential trading opportunities. Traders assess the fundamental factors that can influence the value of the asset, such as company financials, economic indicators, industry trends, and geopolitical factors. They seek to identify undervalued or overvalued assets and make trading decisions based on their assessment of the asset's long-term prospects.

3. Trade Duration: Position traders hold their positions for extended periods, ranging from several weeks to several years. They allow trades to play out over time, aiming to capture the larger price movements associated with the underlying trend.

4. Trend Identification: Position traders focus on identifying and capitalizing on major trends in the market. They look for assets that exhibit clear and sustainable trends, whether it's an uptrend or a downtrend. Trend identification can involve technical

analysis tools, such as trendlines, moving averages, or price patterns, as well as fundamental analysis.

5. Patience and Minimal Intervention: Position traders require patience and discipline, as they often need to withstand periods of price volatility or minor retracements against the overall trend. They avoid frequent trading and minimize unnecessary intervention in their positions, allowing the trade to develop according to their long-term expectations.

6. Risk Management: Position traders employ risk management strategies to protect their capital and manage potential losses. This can include setting appropriate stop-loss orders, diversifying the portfolio across different assets, and position sizing to control the risk exposure of individual trades.

7. Monitoring and Adjustments: While position trading involves longer holding periods, position traders still monitor their positions and make necessary adjustments when new information becomes available or when market conditions change significantly. This can involve revisiting the initial trade thesis, reassessing the fundamentals, or adjusting risk management parameters.

8. Portfolio Allocation: Position traders often build a diversified portfolio of positions across different assets or asset classes. They allocate their capital based on their risk tolerance, market analysis, and long-term investment goals. Portfolio allocation can help spread risk and balance exposure to different market sectors or instruments.

Position trading requires a longer-term commitment and a more strategic approach compared to shorter-term trading strategies. It suits traders or investors who prefer to focus on macro trends, have the patience to wait for profits to materialize over time, and can tolerate potential interim price fluctuations. It's important to conduct thorough research, perform due diligence, and apply proper risk management techniques when engaging in position trading.

CHAPTER 8: TRADING TOOLS AND RESOURCES

8.1 The Importance of Trading Psychology

Trading psychology plays a crucial role in a trader's success. In this section, we emphasize the significance of cultivating a strong trading psychology and mindset. We discuss the psychological challenges faced by traders, such as fear, greed, overconfidence, and impatience. We explore how these emotions can lead to irrational decision-making and negatively impact trading performance. By understanding the importance of trading psychology, you can develop strategies to manage emotions effectively and make rational, disciplined trading decisions.

8.2 Developing Emotional Discipline

Emotional discipline is the ability to control emotions and adhere to a well-defined trading plan. In this section, we delve into the process of developing emotional discipline. We discuss the importance of self-awareness and understanding individual emotional triggers. We explore techniques for managing emotions, such as deep breathing exercises, visualization, and cognitive reframing. Additionally, we highlight the significance of maintaining discipline in executing trades, following risk management protocols, and avoiding impulsive decisions. By developing emotional discipline, you can overcome emotional biases and maintain a focused, rational approach to trading.

8.3 Building a Trading Plan

A well-defined trading plan is essential for success in the financial markets. In this section, we explore the process of building a comprehensive trading plan. We discuss the components of a trading plan, including defining trading goals, selecting trading strategies, establishing risk management guidelines, and setting performance metrics. We also emphasize the importance of documenting the trading plan and regularly reviewing and updating it as needed. By building a robust trading plan, you can maintain clarity and consistency in your trading approach, reducing the impact of emotional decision-making.

8.4 Managing Risk and Capital

Effective risk management is a fundamental aspect of trading. In this section, we focus on managing risk and capital. We discuss the importance of defining risk tolerance and establishing risk-reward ratios for trades. We explore techniques for setting stop-loss orders, position sizing, and diversification. Additionally, we emphasize the significance of preserving capital and avoiding overexposure to high-risk trades. By managing risk and capital effectively, you can protect your trading account from significant losses and ensure long-term sustainability.

8.5 Overcoming Trading Challenges

Trading is not without its challenges, and overcoming obstacles is an essential part of a trader's journey. In this section, we address common trading challenges and provide strategies for overcoming them. We discuss the impact of market volatility, unexpected news events, and trading mistakes. We explore techniques for maintaining resilience in the face of losses or drawdowns and learning from mistakes. Additionally, we highlight the importance of perseverance and adapting to changing market conditions. By overcoming trading challenges, you can develop the resilience and skills necessary to navigate the ups and downs of the market successfully.

CHAPTER 9: BUILDING A SUCCESSFUL TRADING ROUTINE

9.1 The Role of Market Analysis

Market analysis plays a crucial role in trading and investing by providing insights into the current and future market conditions. It involves the examination and interpretation of various factors that influence price movements and market trends. Here's an explanation of the role of market analysis:

1. Understanding Market Trends: Market analysis helps traders and investors understand the overall trend of the market, whether it's bullish (upward), bearish (downward), or range-bound (sideways). By identifying the prevailing trend, traders can align their trading strategies accordingly, whether it's trend following, countertrend, or range trading.

2. Price Analysis: Market analysis involves analyzing price charts and patterns to identify key support and resistance levels, trendlines, chart formations, and other technical indicators. Price analysis helps traders make decisions based on historical price behavior and anticipate potential future price movements.

3. Fundamental Analysis: Fundamental analysis examines the underlying factors that influence an asset's value, such as economic indicators, company financials, industry trends, geopolitical events, and news releases. Traders and investors use fundamental analysis to assess the intrinsic value of an asset and make informed trading decisions based on its fundamental prospects.

4. Market Sentiment: Market analysis helps gauge market sentiment, which refers to the overall psychological

and emotional attitude of market participants towards a particular asset or the market as a whole. Sentiment analysis involves monitoring indicators like investor sentiment surveys, news sentiment, social media sentiment, and options market sentiment. Understanding market sentiment can provide insights into potential market reversals or trends.

5. Technical Indicators: Market analysis incorporates various technical indicators, such as moving averages, oscillators, volume analysis, and trend indicators, to analyze price and volume data. These indicators help identify potential entry and exit points, confirm trends, generate trading signals, and assess the strength or weakness of price movements.

6. Market News and Events: Market analysis includes staying informed about significant news releases, economic events, central bank announcements, geopolitical developments, and other factors that can impact the financial markets. Traders analyze the impact of news and events on market sentiment, volatility, and potential trading opportunities.

7. Risk Assessment: Market analysis is essential for evaluating and managing risk. Traders assess the potential risks and rewards of a trade by analyzing market conditions, volatility levels, correlations, and historical data. This helps in setting appropriate stop-loss levels, position sizing, and risk management strategies.

8. Timing and Market Entry: Market analysis aids in determining the timing of market entry and exit. By analyzing market conditions and using technical or fundamental analysis, traders can identify optimal entry points with favorable risk-reward ratios. Market analysis also helps in identifying potential trend

reversals or periods of consolidation.

9. Decision-Making: Market analysis provides the information and insights necessary for informed decision-making. Traders and investors use market analysis to assess the probability of success, identify potential opportunities, and manage their trades effectively. It helps in formulating trading strategies, adjusting positions, and taking advantage of market inefficiencies.

10. Strategy Development: Market analysis is the foundation for developing trading strategies. Traders use market analysis to identify patterns, trends, and correlations that can be exploited for profit. It helps in selecting appropriate indicators, timeframes, and trading styles that align with market conditions and individual trading objectives.

Market analysis is a continuous process that requires staying informed, utilizing various analytical tools and techniques, and adapting to changing market conditions. It provides valuable insights for traders and investors, enabling them to make informed decisions, manage risk, and optimize their trading strategies.

9.2 Fundamental Analysis

Fundamental analysis is a method of evaluating the intrinsic value of an asset, such as a stock, bond, or commodity, by analyzing the underlying factors that can impact its price. It involves examining the fundamental characteristics of an asset, including its financial health, industry position, management team, and economic environment. Here's an explanation of fundamental analysis:

1. Financial Statements: Fundamental analysis relies on studying financial statements, including balance sheets, income statements, and cash flow statements, to assess

the financial health and performance of a company. Traders and investors analyze metrics such as revenue, earnings, profit margins, debt levels, and cash flow to understand the company's profitability, growth potential, and financial stability.

2. Company and Industry Analysis: Fundamental analysis involves analyzing the company's business model, competitive advantages, market position, and management team. Evaluating the company's products or services, its industry dynamics, and its ability to generate sustainable earnings growth is crucial. Understanding the competitive landscape and industry trends helps assess the company's future prospects.

3. Economic Analysis: Fundamental analysis considers macroeconomic factors that can influence the performance of an asset or a company. This includes analyzing economic indicators such as GDP growth, inflation rates, interest rates, employment data, and consumer spending. Economic analysis helps assess the overall economic environment and its potential impact on the asset being analyzed.

4. Industry Comparison: Comparing a company's financial metrics and performance with its industry peers is an important aspect of fundamental analysis. Traders and investors assess factors like market share, growth rates, profitability ratios, and other industry-specific metrics to understand how a company is positioned relative to its competitors. This comparison helps evaluate a company's competitive advantage and growth potential.

5. Qualitative Factors: Fundamental analysis goes beyond numbers and includes qualitative factors. This involves evaluating a company's management team, corporate governance, brand reputation, intellectual property, regulatory environment, and other qualitative aspects

that can impact its future prospects. Understanding these qualitative factors provides a holistic view of the company's operations and potential risks.

6. Valuation Methods: Fundamental analysis involves valuing an asset to determine whether it is overvalued or undervalued. Common valuation methods include price-to-earnings (P/E) ratio, price-to-sales (P/S) ratio, price-to-book (P/B) ratio, discounted cash flow (DCF) analysis, and comparable company analysis. These methods help assess whether the current price of an asset reflects its underlying value.

7. Catalysts and Events: Fundamental analysis considers upcoming catalysts and events that can impact the asset's value. This includes factors such as product launches, earnings announcements, regulatory changes, industry disruptions, or geopolitical events. Traders and investors assess the potential impact of these events on the asset's price and adjust their investment decisions accordingly.

8. Long-Term Focus: Fundamental analysis takes a long-term perspective, aiming to identify assets with strong fundamentals that can generate sustainable value over time. It is often used by value investors who seek assets that are trading below their intrinsic value, with the expectation that the market will eventually recognize their worth.

Fundamental analysis is particularly relevant for long-term investors who aim to understand the underlying factors that drive an asset's value. It helps traders and investors make informed decisions based on the financial health, industry dynamics, and economic environment. However, it's important to note that fundamental analysis is just one approach, and combining it with other analysis techniques, such as technical analysis, can provide a more comprehensive view of the market.

9.3 Technical Analysis

Technical analysis is a method of analyzing financial markets and making trading decisions based on the historical price and volume data of an asset. It focuses on studying price patterns, trends, support and resistance levels, and various technical indicators to forecast future price movements. Here's an explanation of technical analysis:

1. Price Patterns: Technical analysis involves identifying and analyzing recurring price patterns on charts. Common patterns include head and shoulders, double tops and bottoms, triangles, and flags. These patterns provide insights into potential future price movements, such as trend reversals or continuation patterns.

2. Trend Analysis: Traders use technical analysis to identify trends in the market. This involves studying the direction and strength of price movements over time. Trends can be classified as uptrends (higher highs and higher lows), downtrends (lower highs and lower lows), or sideways trends (range-bound). Trend analysis helps traders determine the overall market sentiment and align their trading strategies accordingly.

3. Support and Resistance Levels: Technical analysis focuses on identifying key support and resistance levels on price charts. Support levels are price levels where buying pressure is expected to be strong enough to prevent further price declines. Resistance levels are price levels where selling pressure is expected to be strong enough to prevent further price increases. These levels help traders identify potential entry or exit points and set stop-loss orders.

4. Technical Indicators: Technical analysis incorporates various technical indicators to analyze price and volume data. These indicators include moving averages,

oscillators (such as RSI, MACD, and Stochastic), volume indicators, and trend indicators. These tools help traders identify overbought or oversold conditions, confirm price trends, generate trading signals, and assess market strength or weakness.

5. Chart Types: Technical analysis utilizes different types of charts, such as line charts, bar charts, and candlestick charts, to visualize price data. Candlestick charts are particularly popular among technical analysts due to their ability to display price patterns and provide insights into market sentiment. Traders use these charts to identify patterns, support and resistance levels, and other technical signals.

6. Timeframes: Technical analysis can be applied to various timeframes, such as intraday, daily, weekly, or monthly charts. Traders select the timeframe that aligns with their trading style and objectives. Short-term traders may focus on intraday or daily charts for quick trades, while long-term investors may analyze weekly or monthly charts for a broader view.

7. Historical Price Data: Technical analysis relies on historical price data to identify patterns, trends, and indicators. Traders analyze past price behavior to understand market dynamics, identify repeating patterns, and make predictions about future price movements. Historical data provides insights into market psychology and helps traders anticipate potential support and resistance levels.

8. Probability and Risk Management: Technical analysis does not provide certainty but focuses on assessing probabilities. Traders use technical analysis to identify high-probability trading opportunities that offer favorable risk-reward ratios. Risk management techniques, such as setting stop-loss orders and position

sizing, are crucial to manage potential losses and control risk exposure.

9. Back testing and Validation: Traders often back test their trading strategies using historical data to assess their effectiveness. Back testing involves applying trading rules to historical price data to evaluate the strategy's performance. Traders also validate their strategies by monitoring real-time trades and adjusting their approach based on ongoing market observations.

10. Integration with Other Analysis Techniques: Technical analysis can be used in conjunction with other forms of analysis, such as fundamental analysis or sentiment analysis. Combining multiple analysis techniques provides a more comprehensive view of the market and helps traders make more informed trading decisions.

Technical analysis is widely used by traders and investors to identify trends, patterns, and potential trading opportunities. It is based on the assumption that historical price patterns and indicators can provide insights into future price movements. However, it's important to note that technical analysis has its limitations and may not always accurately predict market movements. Therefore, it is advisable to combine technical analysis with other forms of analysis and risk management techniques to make well-informed trading decisions.

9.4 Market Sentiment Analysis

Market sentiment analysis refers to the process of assessing and gauging the overall psychological and emotional attitude of market participants towards a particular asset, market, or financial instrument. It involves analyzing the collective sentiment, opinions, and beliefs of traders and investors to understand their expectations and assess the potential direction of future price movements. Here's an explanation of market sentiment analysis:

1. Indicators of Market Sentiment: Market sentiment can be inferred from various indicators and sources, including:

    - News Sentiment: Analyzing news articles, headlines, and reports to identify positive or negative sentiment towards a specific asset or market. This can involve monitoring news sentiment through automated tools or sentiment analysis algorithms.

    - Social Media Sentiment: Monitoring social media platforms, forums, and online communities to gauge public sentiment and discussions related to a particular asset or market. This can involve analyzing keywords, hashtags, or sentiment scores from social media data.

    - Options Market Sentiment: Assessing the sentiment reflected in the options market, including options pricing, open interest, and trading volume. High call option volume or a large number of put options being traded may indicate bullish or bearish sentiment, respectively.

    - Investor Sentiment Surveys: Reviewing sentiment surveys conducted among investors and traders to gauge their outlook, confidence, and sentiment towards the market or specific assets.

    - Technical Indicators: Certain technical indicators, such as the relative strength index (RSI), can provide insights into overbought or oversold conditions in the market, which can reflect sentiment extremes.

2. Bullish and Bearish Sentiment: Market sentiment can be

classified as bullish (positive) or bearish (negative):

- Bullish Sentiment: Bullish sentiment indicates an optimistic outlook towards the market or a specific asset. It suggests that market participants anticipate rising prices or positive market conditions. It may be driven by positive economic data, favorable news, or anticipation of strong earnings.

- Bearish Sentiment: Bearish sentiment reflects a pessimistic outlook towards the market or a specific asset. It suggests that market participants expect declining prices or negative market conditions. It may be driven by negative news, economic uncertainties, or concerns about geopolitical events.

3. Impact on Market Movements: Market sentiment can influence buying and selling decisions, which can impact price movements. When market sentiment is overwhelmingly bullish, it may lead to increased buying activity and upward price pressure. Conversely, when market sentiment is bearish, it may result in selling pressure and downward price movements.

4. Contrarian Approach: Contrarian traders often use market sentiment analysis as a tool to identify potential market reversals. They believe that extreme sentiment levels, such as excessive optimism or pessimism, can indicate an overbought or oversold market and may lead to a reversal in price direction. Contrarian traders may take positions opposite to prevailing sentiment.

5. Integration with Other Analysis Techniques: Market sentiment analysis is often used in conjunction with other forms of analysis, such as fundamental analysis or technical analysis. Combining multiple analysis techniques provides a more comprehensive view of the

market and helps traders make more informed trading decisions.

6. Limitations: Market sentiment analysis has limitations, as sentiment alone does not guarantee market movements. It is a subjective measure that can change quickly, and market sentiment indicators can sometimes be influenced by noise or short-term factors. Therefore, it's important to consider sentiment analysis as one tool among many in the trading decision-making process.

Market sentiment analysis provides insights into the collective psychology and emotions of market participants, allowing traders and investors to understand prevailing attitudes and potential market movements. By assessing market sentiment, traders can make more informed decisions, identify potential trading opportunities, and manage risk effectively.

9.5 Research and Information Sources

Research and information sources are essential for traders and investors to gather reliable and relevant data that can inform their decision-making process. These sources provide access to market data, news, analysis, and other information necessary for understanding the financial markets. Here's an explanation of research and information sources commonly used in trading:

1. Financial News Websites: Financial news websites, such as Bloomberg, Reuters, CNBC, and Financial Times, provide up-to-date news, market analysis, economic data, and insights into various financial markets. These websites offer a wide range of information on stocks, bonds, currencies, commodities, and global market trends.

2. Market Data Platforms: Market data platforms, such as Bloomberg Terminal, Thomson Reuters Eikon, and

FactSet, provide real-time and historical market data, including prices, volume, volatility, and other relevant metrics. These platforms offer comprehensive tools for analyzing market trends, creating charts, and conducting in-depth research.

3. Company Filings and Reports: Traders and investors can access company filings and reports through regulatory bodies like the U.S. Securities and Exchange Commission (SEC) or financial information providers such as EDGAR (Electronic Data Gathering, Analysis, and Retrieval system). These filings include financial statements, annual reports, and other disclosures that provide insights into a company's operations, performance, and potential risks.

4. Earnings Releases and Conference Calls: Earnings releases and conference calls are key sources of information for publicly traded companies. Companies announce their quarterly or annual earnings results, providing insights into their financial performance, outlook, and management commentary. Investors can access this information through company websites, financial news platforms, or investor relations portals.

5. Research Reports: Research reports prepared by investment banks, brokerage firms, and independent research providers offer in-depth analysis, recommendations, and insights on specific companies, sectors, or markets. These reports often include financial models, valuation analysis, and fundamental assessments that can assist traders and investors in making informed decisions.

6. Economic Data Releases: Government agencies and central banks regularly release economic data that provide insights into the health and performance of economies. Economic indicators, such as GDP growth,

employment data, inflation rates, and interest rates, can significantly impact financial markets. Traders and investors can access economic data through government websites, central bank publications, or financial news platforms.

7. Social Media and Online Communities: Social media platforms, forums, and online communities can provide valuable insights, discussions, and opinions about specific assets or market trends. Traders can participate in online communities, follow influential market participants, and engage in discussions to gather alternative viewpoints and stay updated on market sentiment.

8. Financial Analysis Platforms and Tools: Various online platforms and tools provide financial analysis, screening capabilities, and technical charting features. Examples include Trading View, Finviz, Stock Charts, and Yahoo Finance. These platforms allow users to analyze stock prices, technical indicators, screen for specific criteria, and generate trading ideas.

9. Academic Research and Journals: Academic research papers and journals can provide in-depth studies and analysis on specific financial topics, trading strategies, and market dynamics. Scholars and researchers publish their findings in academic journals like the Journal of Finance, Journal of Financial Economics, and the Journal of Portfolio Management.

10. Professional Networks and Conferences: Engaging with industry professionals, attending conferences, and participating in professional networks can provide valuable insights and access to industry experts. Networking with fellow traders, attending seminars, webinars, or industry events can facilitate knowledge sharing and foster valuable connections.

Traders and investors should use a combination of these research and information sources to gather a diverse range of perspectives and make well-informed decisions. It's important to consider the reliability, credibility, and relevance of the sources and continuously evaluate and update the information used for trading and investment purposes.

CHAPTER 10: CONCLUSION

10.1 Recap of Key Concepts

In this final chapter, we recap the key concepts covered in the book "The Art of Trading: Insider Tips for Stock Exchange Profits." We have journeyed through various aspects of trading, including understanding the stock exchange, developing a trading plan, analyzing the markets, implementing trading strategies, managing risk, and cultivating a resilient mindset. We have explored fundamental and technical analysis techniques, discussed different trading strategies, and emphasized the importance of risk management and trade psychology.

10.2 The Importance of Continuous Learning

Trading is a dynamic and ever-evolving field. It is essential to recognize that learning is a continuous process. Markets change, new trading techniques emerge, and staying updated with the latest trends and developments is crucial for long-term success. As traders, we must commit to ongoing education, reading books, attending seminars, and staying connected with the trading community. The more knowledge and skills we acquire, the better equipped we are to adapt to changing market conditions and seize profitable opportunities.

10.3 The Role of Practice and Experience

While theory is valuable, practice and experience are equally vital components of becoming a successful trader. It is essential to put the knowledge gained into action by actively participating in the markets. Through real-world trading, we gain practical insights, learn from our mistakes, and refine our strategies. It is important to start with small positions and gradually increase exposure as confidence and competence grow. By immersing ourselves in the trading process, we develop a deeper understanding of market dynamics and enhance our ability to make informed decisions.

10.4 The Discipline of Risk Management

Throughout the book, we have emphasized the critical role of risk management in trading. It is the bedrock upon which successful trading strategies are built. Implementing effective risk management practices allows us to protect our capital, minimize losses during unfavorable market conditions, and maintain long-term sustainability. By setting risk parameters, employing risk mitigation techniques, and managing the psychological aspects of risk, we increase the likelihood of achieving consistent profits while preserving capital.

10.5 The Power of Trade Psychology

Trade psychology is often overlooked but plays a significant role in trading success. Mastering our emotions, maintaining discipline, and developing a resilient mindset are essential components of becoming a successful trader. By managing emotions such as fear, greed, and impatience, we can make rational trading decisions and avoid impulsive behavior that can lead to significant losses. Cultivating a growth mindset, learning from losses, and staying focused on long-term goals are key factors in overcoming challenges and achieving consistent profitability.

10.6 The Journey Ahead

As we conclude this book, it is important to acknowledge that the journey as a trader is ongoing. The financial markets are dynamic, and there is always more to learn and explore. It is crucial to adapt to changing market conditions, stay updated with the latest trading techniques and strategies, and continually refine our skills. The road to trading success may have its ups and downs, but with dedication, perseverance, and continuous learning, we can navigate the challenges and achieve our financial goals.